REGULATORY CHANGE IN AN ATMOSPHERE OF CRISIS

Current Implications of the Roosevelt Years

REGULATORY CHANGE IN AN ATMOSPHERE OF CRISIS

Current Implications of the Roosevelt Years

Edited by

Gary M. Walton

Dean and Professor of Economics
College of Business and Economics
Washington State University
Pullman, Washington

 1979

ACADEMIC PRESS
A Subsidiary of Harcourt Brace Jovanovich, Publishers
New York   London   Toronto   Sydney   San Francisco

COPYRIGHT © 1979, BY ACADEMIC PRESS, INC.
ALL RIGHTS RESERVED.
NO PART OF THIS PUBLICATION MAY BE REPRODUCED OR
TRANSMITTED IN ANY FORM OR BY ANY MEANS, ELECTRONIC
OR MECHANICAL, INCLUDING PHOTOCOPY, RECORDING, OR ANY
INFORMATION STORAGE AND RETRIEVAL SYSTEM, WITHOUT
PERMISSION IN WRITING FROM THE PUBLISHER.

ACADEMIC PRESS, INC.
111 Fifth Avenue, New York, New York 10003

United Kingdom Edition published by
ACADEMIC PRESS, INC. (LONDON) LTD.
24/28 Oval Road, London NW1 7DX

Library of Congress Cataloging in Publication Data
Main entry under title:

Regulatory change in an atmosphere of crisis.

    Proceedings of a conference held Apr. 27–29, 1978,
at Washington State University.
    Includes bibliographies and index.
    1. United States--Economic policy--1933–1945--
Congresses. 2. United States--Economic policy--
1971-   --Congresses. I. Walton, Gary M.
II. Title.
HC106.3.R464   330.9'73'0917   79–23164
ISBN 0–12–733950–7

PRINTED IN THE UNITED STATES OF AMERICA

79 80 81 82   9 8 7 6 5 4 3 2 1

*TO MYRTLE WALTON
AND THE MEMORY OF MYRTLE NEBECKER*

Contents

LIST OF CONTRIBUTORS	xi
PREFACE	xiii

Chapter 1
Monetary Crises and Government Reliance in Modern Times — 1
Gary M. Walton

The Great Crisis of the 1930s	1
Permitting the Great Crisis	4
The Mandate for Security	5
Today's Monetary Crisis	7
Wage and Price Controls: A Political Diversion	8
Today's Monetary Crisis and the Tax Revolt	9
Conclusion	10
References	11

Chapter 2
The Economic Constitution and the New Deal: Lessons for Late Learners — 13
James M. Buchanan

Constitutional Failure	13
What Might Have Been	15
What Was	17
What Is	20
Implications for Reform	24
References	26

Discussion — 27
Robert W. Clower

Chapter 3
Roots of Regulation: The New Deal — 31
Jonathan Hughes

The Entrepreneurial Government Firm	33
Subsidies and Expenditures	34
Federal Establishment of Unions	41
Agency Nonmarket Controls	44
Social Insurance	49
Conclusions	52
References	53

Discussion — 57
Peter Temin

Chapter 4
The Robinson-Patman Act: A New Deal for Small Business — 63
Kenneth G. Elzinga

Robinson-Patman as New Deal Legislation	64
Robinson-Patman Act as Precursor of Regulatory Reform	67
Economic Analysis and Price Discrimination Policy	69
A Time for Change	71
References	73

Discussion — 75
Victor P. Goldberg

Chapter 5
Banking Reform in the 1930s — 79
Homer Jones

Introduction	79
The 1933–1935 Reforms	79
Statistical Behavior of the Money Stock 1919–1976	83
The Last Twenty Years—The 1933–1935 Reforms in Perspective	84
Conclusions	89
References	90

Discussion — 93
Anna J. Schwartz

Changes for Commercial and Savings Banks	93
Changes with Respect to the Federal Reserve System	97
Summary	98
References	99

Chapter 6
On Understanding the Birth and Evolution of the Securities and Exchange Commission: Where Are We in the Theory of Regulation?   **101**
Robert J. MacKay and Joseph D. Reid, Jr.

Introduction	101
Theories of Economic Regulation	102
The Birth of the SEC and the Explanatory Power of Alternative Theories of Regulation	108
Recent Regulatory Reform by the SEC and the Explanatory Power of Alternative Theories of Regulation	115
Conclusion	118
References	119

Discussion   **123**
George J. Benston

Chapter 7
Taxes, Transfers, and Income Inequality   **129**
Edgar K. Browning and William R. Johnson

Description of Data	130
The Tax System	132
Taxes and Transfer	137
Evaluating Income Inequality	142
Conclusion	148
Appendix	148
References	151

Discussion   **153**
Thomas E. Borcherding

SUBJECT INDEX   161

List of Contributors

Numbers in parentheses indicate the pages on which the authors' contributions begin.

George J. Benston (123), Department of Economics, University of Rochester, Rochester, New York 14627

Thomas E. Borcherding (153), Department of Economics, Simon Fraser University, Burnaby, British Columbia, Canada

Edgar K. Browning (129), Department of Economics, University of Virginia, Charlottesville, Virginia 22903

James M. Buchanan (13), Department of Economics, Virginia Polytechnic Institute and State University, Blacksburg, Virginia 24061

Robert W. Clower (27), Department of Economics, University of California, Los Angeles, Los Angeles, California 90024

Kenneth G. Elzinga (63), Department of Economics, University of Virginia, Charlottesville, Virginia 22903

Victor P. Goldberg (75), Department of Economics, University of California, Davis, Davis, California 95616

Jonathan Hughes (31), Department of Economics, Northwestern University, Evanston, Illinois 60201

William R. Johnson (129), Department of Economics, University of California, Los Angeles, Los Angeles, California 90024

Homer Jones (79), Yorkshire Place, St. Louis, Missouri 63119

Robert J. MacKay (101), Center for the Study of Public Choice, Virginia Polytechnic Institute and State University, Blacksburg, Virginia 24061

Joseph D. Reid, Jr.* (101), Center for the Study of Public Choice, Virginia Polytechnic Institute and State University, Blacksburg, Virginia 24061

Anna J. Schwartz (93), National Bureau of Economic Research Inc., New York, New York 10012

*PRESENT ADDRESS: Department of Economics, Virginia Polytechnic Institute and State University, Blacksburg, Va. 24061.

Peter Temin (57), Department of Economics, Massachusetts Institute of Technology, Cambridge, Massachusetts 02139

Gary M. Walton (1), College of Business and Economics, Washington State University, Pullman, Washington 99164

Preface

The Great Depression of the 1930s was undoubtedly one of the great watersheds of history, not only for the United States, but for many other nations as well. Understandably, extensive scholarly effort has been given to the study of the causes of the economic collapse and subsequent recovery. Unfortunately, it is too often forgotten that a host of economic reforms, many revolutionary in character, transpired in the United States during the Roosevelt years. Most of those incipient regulations and extensions of government control did not appear revolutionary in their early forms, and undoubtedly the long-run outcome of those changes were not foreseen. However, it is now apparent that the rapid growth of regulation and government control, both then and today, has had serious adverse effects, especially in terms of productive efficiency and individual freedom. If the proliferation of wasteful regulations is to be reversed, it is essential that the initial events that inspired them be understood. Moreover, this must be accomplished in conjunction with an analysis of the current-day implications of those beginnings.

To advance scholarly inquiry on these issues, a conference, Regulatory Change in an Atmosphere of Crisis: The Current-Day Implications of the Roosevelt Years, was held April 27-29, 1978, at Washington State University. Invited participants came from different backgrounds, from business, government, and academia, and the sessions, as the many in attendance can attest, were extremely lively and rewarding. The papers and discussions were especially provocative and clearly demanded wider dissemination. After appropriate revision and review, and with the addition of one paper (Chapter 1), the papers and discussions were ready for publication.

The purpose of this volume is to communicate scholarly findings on several of the major economic reforms of the Roosevelt years and to assess their current-day implications. The book proceeds from general analyses of the causes and consequences of the economic changes of the period to in-depth analyses of several particular reforms. In combination, the papers and discussions offer a significant contribution to the economic history of the Great Depression as well as to many of the current problems confronting Americans today.

Many individuals contributed to this endeavor, but I am particularly grateful to Richard Larry, Hubert F. Leonard, and Chuck Rossie for their support and advice, and Joy Scott for her editorial assistance.

REGULATORY CHANGE IN AN ATMOSPHERE OF CRISIS
Current Implications of the Roosevelt Years

Chapter 1

Monetary Crises and Government Reliance in Modern Times

GARY M. WALTON

THE GREAT CRISIS OF THE 1930s

Lord Keynes's famous quip that "in the long-run we're all dead" appropriately emphasizes the atmosphere of crisis that prevailed in the 1930s and the need at that time for immediate action—measures that would take effect in the short-run. Anyone familiar with the despair and suffering of the period could hardly disagree, and advice and predictions that the economy would eventually rebound simply imposed irritation on top of hardship.

A brief sketch of aggregate conditions in the 1930s are shown graphically in Figures 1.1–1.3. As indicated, in the years between late 1929 and 1933, the American economy (and all other advanced economies) simply fell apart. The Gross National Product (GNP) in current values tumbled from $104 billion to $56 billion, and in real terms, declined by 31%. Figure 1.2 shows the collapse of investment during these years. By 1933, gross investments were below levels of capital depreciation. The nation's capital stock was actually declining. Wholesale and consumer prices dropped by one-third and one-fourth, respectively, and industrial production fell by one-half. The most alarming statistics of all, however,

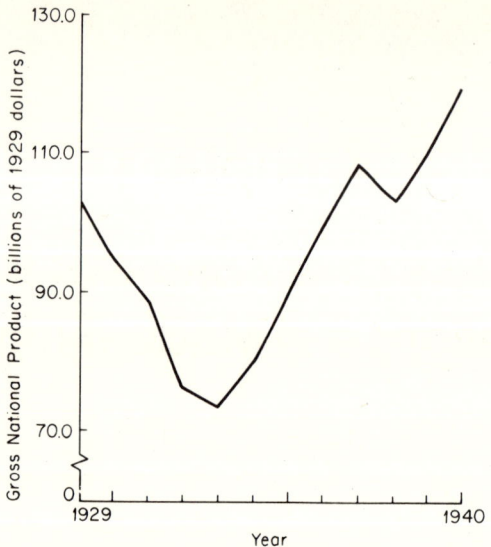

Figure 1.1. Gross National Product for 1929-1940. (Source: J. W. Kendrick, *Productivity Trends in the United States,* National Bureau of Economic Research No. 71, Princeton University Press, Princeton, 1961, p. 291.)

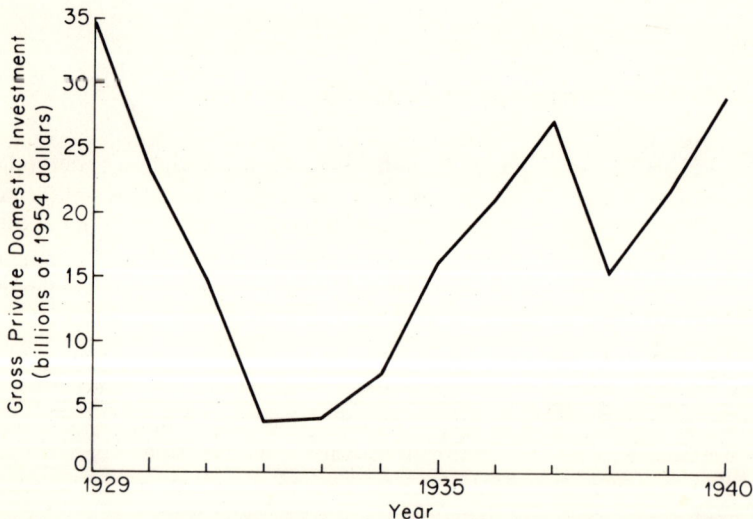

Figure 1.2. Gross private domestic investment for 1929-1940. (Source: U.S. Office of Business Economics, U.S. Income and Output, 1958, p. 118.)

1. Monetary Crises and Government Reliance in Modern Times

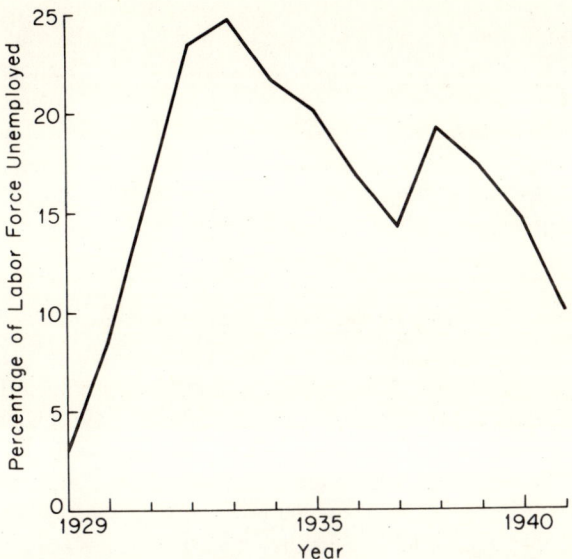

Figure 1.3. Percentage of labor force unemployed for 1929–1940. (Source: *Economic Report of the President,* Jan. 1955, p. 153.)

were those of employment. No one knows the exact count, but nearly 13 million workers were unemployed in 1933. As shown in Figure 1.3, that number represented approximately one-fourth of the civilian workforce.[1]

In short, the crisis was real and immense, and everyone knew it. By the time the economy hit bottom, in 1933, what opportunities for recovery were there? The persistent contraction of markets had imposed a sense of hopelessness and ruin on the agricultural, manufacturing, and service sectors. Even state and local governments faced financial difficulties and forced retrenchment. Of course, the financial sector was in shambles. The nation experienced three extensive bank panics between 1930 and 1933, as people scrambled to convert their deposits into currency. Meanwhile, the Federal Reserve system took no decisive action to correct the downward course. The policies implemented first were a host of federal-assistance programs to preserve the remnants of the economic structure which were still intact in 1933, and other policies were ultimately instituted to increase spending and employment directly.

The New Deal has sometimes been viewed as an attack on the free-enterprise system. While that was not intended initially, the momentum that developed then and later did move the American economy toward an increasing reliance on the public sector. The atmoshphere of crisis that prevailed in 1933 demanded

---

[1] For a correction in the official post-1933 unemployment figures, see Darby, 1976.

bold measures, and decision makers could not realistically consider options between existing levels of government activity and less. Without a strong leadership role from the Federal Reserve only one option remained: more government intervention. Even philosophically, to many, it was not so much a decision for private enterprise vis-á-vis more government controls, as it was between a complete socialist order or a private-enterprise system with more government control and activity. Fears of socialism made the compromise mixture politically palatable at a time when urgent action seemed economically essential.

PERMITTING THE GREAT CRISIS

The initial forces that created the Great Depression have been the subject of repeated analysis and debate (see Freidman and Schwartz, 1963; Galbraith, 1955; Temin, 1976; Meltzer, 1976; and Mayer, 1978). The decline in stock prices, the impact of weather on agricultural prices, monetary policy, and other economic policies operating under the rules of the interwar gold standard are frequently suggested. Whatever the initial causes, they appear to be less important than the fact that no strong counterrecessionary measures were taken in time to correct the recessionary trend.

A multiplicity of interacting forces pushed the economy on its downward course, but the single most important source of contraction, once underway, was the sharp, persistent decline in the money supply. Figure 1.4 shows the changes

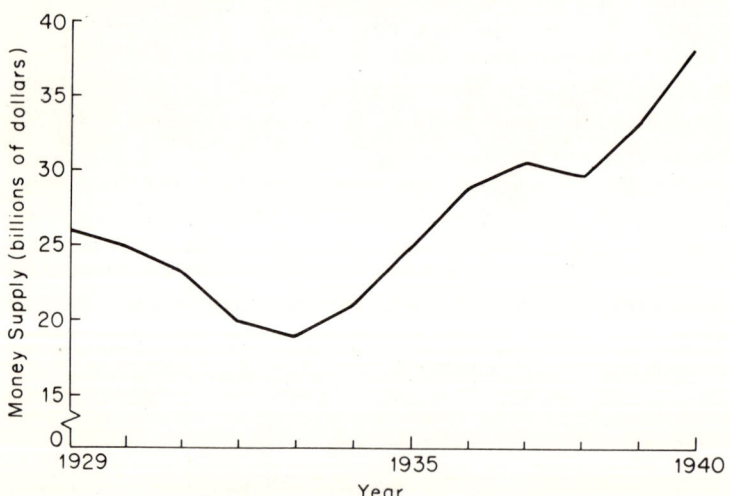

Figure 1.4. Money Supply for 1929–1940. (Source: Board of Governors of the Federal Reserve System, Federal Reserve Bulletin.)

in the nation's money supply throughout the perilous decade, and the failure of the monetary authorities to stop the decline before 1933. Perhaps it is most accurate to say that the Federal Reserve allowed rather than caused the money supply to decrease during the period of bank panics (1930–1933).[2] Some have argued that the Federal Reserve authorities normally have the power to constrain the money supply but not to expand it if banks are unwilling to lend. However, much of the decline in the money supply came from runs on banks with falling capital assets, mainly bonds, and the Federal Reserve certainly had the power to purchase bonds and thereby strengthen the banks' asset values. This would have made banks more solvent, reduced the sense of alarm, and stemmed the tide of bank failures. It also would have enlarged the banks' reserves and the money supply. In any case, a strong expansionary monetary policy sufficient to cushion the fall and hold the crisis to a recession was never attempted. In fact, the Federal Reserve often sold rather than bought bonds.

The failure of the Federal Reserve to meet its responsibilities and to employ strong countercyclical measures before 1933 dealt a crippling blow to a weakening economy. Ironically, without design or intention, one arm of government set the stage for the creation and expansion of others.

THE MANDATE FOR SECURITY

The atmosphere of crisis that accompanied Franklin Roosevelt's sweep into office brought forth a mass of legislation, especially in the first 100 days of his administration. The alphabet-soup listing—NIRA, RFC, AAA, FDIC, WPA, CCC, SEC, TVA, PWZ, NLRB (and others)—characterized the intensity of legislative activity in the early days and thereafter. Many of these measures were intended to protect the surviving businesses of the 1929–1933 period. Others were created to directly help the unemployed. All were part of the quest for security.

The latter point warrants emphasis. With few exceptions, the most distinguishing characteristic of the Roosevelt reforms was their guarantee of economic security rather than the direct increase of aggregate demand. The crisis provided politically sensitive, vested-interest groups with an unusual set of circumstances. Roosevelt had a mandate to take action, and farmers, large corporations, small businesses, banks, organized labor, government bureaucracies (at all levels), and many others sought and won protection through federal legislation. Of course, such attempts were not unprecedented, but the scale of government reliance that resulted was unlike anything that preceded it.

Compared to recent times, the acts of legislation passed during the Roosevelt

---

[2] For an analysis of this failure to take action, see Friedman and Schwartz (1963), Wicker (1965), Brunner and Meltzer (1964), and Meltzer (1976).

years were relatively modest steps toward greater government intervention. However, the effects of those early acts broadened as additions, alterations, and extensions increased and strengthened the bureaucracies created by them. Moreover, the New Deal reforms, which were for the most part redistributive microeconomic policies, rather than countercyclical macroeconomic measures, appeared to turn the economic tide. Their introduction accompanied the post-1933 upturn (see Figures 1.1–1.3) of real GNP, investment, and employment.

As the Federal Reserve authorities continued their above-the-battle stance, new federal funding agencies were formed to act in their place. The rapid growth of the money supply (see Figure 1.4), beginning in late 1933, although passively accommodated by Federal Reserve policy, was not spearheaded by it. It came primarily from the swell of gold reserves precipitated by the 1933 devaluation, the conversion of currency to demand deposits by individuals and businesses, and the upsurge of government-backed loans from the Reconstruction Finance Corporation to banks, state and local governments, and businesses. The Home Owner's Loan Corporation added further loan security by guaranteeing mortgages in urban housing.

Similarly, although federal spending increased after 1933, Roosevelt's fiscal policies of tax and expenditure changes, in combination, were not expansionary.[3] Only in 1937 did fiscal policy contribute positively, but this was more than offset by the monetary contraction initiated by the Federal Reserve's raising of the reserve requirements in 1936 and 1937. It was not until World War II that both monetary policy and fiscal policy were sustained in a strong expansionary way. The result, as we know, was the rapid attainment of full employment.

Any crisis, real or imaginary, is bound to effect change in a significant way. The speed, ultimate level, and duration of the economic collapse of the 1930s were all without precedent. Because of the intensity of the crisis, a mass of legislation was undertaken that, in historical perspective, was likewise unprecedented. Undoubtedly, the magnitude of the crisis generated greater government reaction—once action was taken—than would have occurred in less severe times.

In that sense, the early Roosevelt years were a great watershed in the history of the United States. They precipitated a significant change in approach and attitude toward social ills.[4] That change toward greater reliance on government

---

[3] For evidence and analysis of the absence of strong fiscal policy during the 1930s, see Brown (1956) and Pepper (1973).

[4] I am referring here to what Douglass North (1978) has called "the disintegration of the Madisonian system." North goes on to say that, "The breakdown of the Madisonian political structure was not a consequence of the 'proletarian' losers of the nineteenth century—the indigenous Indian, the ex-slave, or the protests of the Western Federation of Miners, the Molly McGuires, the I.W.W. It was the result of conflicting propertied groups—farmers, shippers, railroad companies, manufacturers subject to foreign competition—all attempting to protect themselves from competition." The change in opportunities to use the political system for gain accelerated in the 1930s. Technological changes such as the telephone and

and less on private initiative and individual responsibility was reinforced by the economic stimulation of massive government spending during World War II, which culminated in the social welfare experiments of the Great Society and programs thereafter. The result was a lasting alteration in opportunities between the public and private sectors for increasing or redistributing wealth.

Milton Friedman (1978) appropriately describes the transition in terms of a relaxation of constitutional restrictions:

> The essential difference was that before 1930 or so there was a widespread belief on the part of the public that government should be limited and that danger arose from the growth of government. President Grover Cleveland maintained, for instance, that while the people should support their government, the government should not support the people. President Woodrow Wilson remarked that the history of liberalism was the history of restraints on government power. Almost everyone then agreed that the role of government was to act as a referee and umpire and not as a Big Brother. Once this fundamental attitude of the public changed, however, constitutional restrictions became very much less effective against the growth of government. As we all know, the Supreme Court does follow the election returns (sometimes tardily) and most of the New Deal measures which were ruled unconstitutional by the Court in President Roosevelt's first administration were ruled to be constitutional in the second administration[5] [Friedman, M. The limitations of tax limitation. *Policy Review,* Summer 1978].

TODAY'S MONETARY CRISIS

The persistently high level of inflation is currently creating an atmosphere of widespread discontent with and distrust in government. There is a growing awareness that the inflation is being caused by government. By mid-1979, 31 states had petitioned Congress to convene a constitutional convention to require by amendment a balanced federal budget.[6] Although some of the support for such an amendment has come from anti-big-government factions, much of it stems from the correct recognition that chronic deficits at the federal level continue out of control. Persistent deficits, sometimes in excess of $50 billion, are commonplace, and repeated claims that they will be reduced and eventually eliminated fail to come true. Likewise, the federal government's periodic attempts to contain inflation since its upsurge in 1966 have been systematically abandoned. This has resulted in a loss of confidence in the government's credibility on this issue.

---

the airplane and others such as tax write-offs may have lowered the costs of lobbying, but also important was the new sympathetic ear of an alarmed legislature and administration willing to respond to pleas for help.

[5] Buchanan enlarges on this point in the following chapter.

[6] Before such a convention can be called, thirty-four states must pass a resolution calling for it.

Today's inflation is not caused by labor unions, oil sheiks, other monopolists, or a new outburst of human greed. It is caused by the creation of excessive amounts of money. The central problem is that the growth of federal spending, relative to taxes, has been accompanied almost automatically by increases in the money supply. As was characteristic of World War II policies, the Federal Reserve systematically purchases U.S. bonds in open-market operations, thus helping the Treasury to finance federal deficits. As a result the money supply increases.

The fundamental law of economics cannot be repealed, even by government: If something rapidly increases in supply (relative to demand), its relative value will fall. The rapid increase in dollars relative to goods leads to a fall in the value of the dollar. Inflation is an example of the law at work. The only effective cure for inflation is to control the money supply. Without the political will to do it, today's monetary crisis will continue to mount.

WAGE AND PRICE CONTROLS: A POLITICAL DIVERSION

Recognizing inflation as the number-one economic problem today, Jimmy Carter has called for voluntary wage and price controls. Such measures are futile and counterproductive. However, they do have the political effect of shifting the responsibility for inflation from the government to the private sector.

Although few believe that Carter's program of voluntary restraints will work, a recent Gallup poll indicates that a majority of Americans mistakenly believe that another try at mandatory wage-price controls is the only hope. The last time public support for wage and price controls exceeded 50% was late in the summer of 1971, when Richard Nixon announced Phase I of his control program.

A 10-year history of recent price movements and the effects of Nixon's controls on inflation are displayed in Figure 1.5. The precontrol peak of inflation,

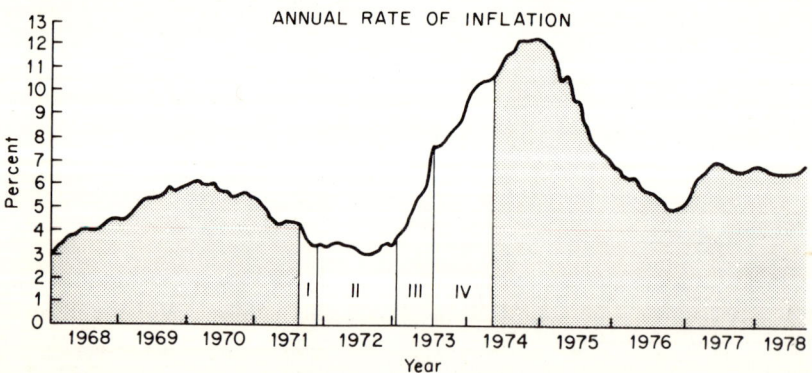

Figure 1.5. Annual rate of inflation for 1968–1978. (Source: U.S. Department of Commerce Statistical Abstract, 1978, p. 483.)

at 6% annually, came in early 1970; then inflation gradually fell to 4.5% by August, 1971, when Nixon imposed a 90-day wage-price freeze. Clearly, the freeze was evasive and incomplete, but the growth of prices was moderated somewhat through the first and second phases of controls. While some may believe that the lower rate of inflation was due to the controls, it was actually due to the delayed influence of restrictive monetary measures in 1969 and 1970. By late 1972, despite the controls, renewed rapid growth of the money supply was pressing prices upward at a faster rate. When controls were finally lifted, on April 30, 1974, inflation was in excess of 10%. In summary, when controls began, the rate of inflation was 4.5% and falling; when controls ended, the rate was 10% and rising.

Rather than helpful, controls are actually inflationary. Not only do they impose direct waste by utilizing millions of government and industry labor hours for futile policing and administration, but they also create sizable indirect costs. As market conditions change, unresponsive rigid prices begin to impose shortages, distortions, and other inefficiencies. During the period of Nixon's controls, fertilizer and chemical firms sidestepped sales at artificially low prices in domestic markets by increasing exports. This impinged negatively on agricultural production, lowering supplies and pressing food prices upward. Since prices of imports were not frozen, United States lumber firms first shipped wood products to Canada, and then returned them for sale in the United States. Because poultry feed prices were not subject to controls, it became unprofitable to raise chickens for sale at fixed government prices; hence poultry growers slaughtered chicks by the millions. Similar examples of circumvention and waste abound, from added fat on meat to lower work effort due to fixed money wages. In short, because controls prevent the price mechanism from coordinating markets, inefficiencies lower supply and add to the problem of inflation.

The aforementioned record mirrors earlier attempts to fight inflation by government controls. They never work, because they attack symptoms rather than causes. It is analogous to trying to stop steam escaping from a boiling teapot by plugging the spout; the only way to stop the steam is to turn down the heat. The only way to reduce the rate of inflation is to restrain the expansion of the money supply and reduce the size and persistence of federal deficits.

TODAY'S MONETARY CRISIS AND THE TAX REVOLT

Only recently has there developed serious political support for a pause in this persistent dependence on government. Today's rallying cry against big government, unresponsive centralized controls, inflation, and high taxes is gathering momentum. Such prominent national figures as Governors Jerry Brown, of California, James Thompson, of Illinois, and Dixie Lee Ray, of Washington, who originally opposed tax-revolt measures, have altered their position. Further, the major, most-discussed issue in the November, 1978, national elections was economy in government.

The growing concern about waste in government was given a critical political nudge in California by a mini-crisis. Property values, both market and assessed, approximately doubled between 1973 and 1978. This rise was propelled by general inflation, but was further heightened by immigration, by environmental restrictions, and by purchases of property as hedges against inflation. The acceleration of property values was paralleled by soaring property taxes, and some claimed that many homeowners would default on payments and be forced to sell. The passage of Proposition 13, in June, 1978, radically cut property taxes and, by requiring a two-thirds-majority vote for new or higher taxes, made it significantly more difficult to substitute other taxes.

Proponents of limited government, on philosophical or other grounds, were important to the passage of Proposition 13, but three similar measures had been rejected in California in the previous 15 years; therefore proponents of property tax relief were essential supporters for its passage. Although the California crisis in property taxes, which stemmed from the unexpected, rapid acceleration of property values, has been solved, at least temporarily, the far more significant crisis of inflation continues to grow apace.

CONCLUSION

The monetary crisis of the 1930s was, of course, far more serious than that of today. Nevertheless, expectations and attitudes are changing, and further delay in appropriate action to halt inflation will intensify the crisis. For this reason also, wage and price controls are counterproductive. Moreover, the greater the delay in taking appropriate monetary action, the greater will be the governmental reaction (as was the case in the 1930s), whatever form it may take.

The central purpose of the following collection of essays is to assess several reforms that were central to the "reaction" of the great crisis of the 1930s. To a significant degree the spirit of that reaction has persisted. Acts of legislation similar to Roosevelt's early reforms have moved the American economy increasingly toward a controlled one. Yet, there is growing awareness that the economy is out of control.

As in the 1930s, the agency primarily responsible for this sense of alarm is the Federal Reserve. Whether today's political reaction will also lead to more controls, such as Carter's wage and price controls, or whether less government reliance, in the spirit of the tax revolt, will result is for the future to tell. The lessons of this volume would indicate a need to eliminate those regulations and controls which stifle competition and production. Controls affect the general price level only indirectly and usually adversely. Responsibility for the 1930s deflation and today's inflation lies with misguided Federal Reserve policy.

ACKNOWLEDGMENT

I am grateful to Douglass C. North, Karl Brunner, Roger L. Miller, Carolyn Clark, Stan Smith, Eugene Clark and Philip Coelho for their advice and criticisms of an earlier draft of this paper.

REFERENCES

Brown, E. C. Fiscal policy in the thirties: A reappraisal. *American Economic Review*, Dec. 1956, 857–879.

Brunner, K., and Meltzer, A. H. *The Federal Reserve's attachment to free reserves.* (Prepared for Banking and Currency Committee, U.S. House of Representatives.) Washington, D.C., 1964.

Darby, M. R. Three-and-a-half million U.S. employees have been mislaid: Or an explanation of unemployment, 1934–1941. *Journal of Political Economy*, 1976, *84*, 1-16.

Friedman, M. The limitations of tax limitation. *Policy Review*, Summer 1978.

Friedman, M., and Schwartz, A. J. *A monetary history of the United States, 1867-1960.* National Bureau of Economic Research, Princeton University Press, Princeton 1961.

Galbraith, J. K. *The great crash.* Boston: Houghton-Mifflin, 1955.

Mayer, T. Money and the Great Depression: A Critique of Professor Temin's thesis. *Explorations in Economics History*, 1978, *15*, 127-145.

Meltzer, A. H. Monetary and other explanations of the Great Depression. *Journal of Monetary Economics*, 1976, *2*, 455-471.

North, D. Structure and performance: The task of economic history. *Journal of Economic Literature*, 1978, *XVI*, 970-971.

Pepper, L. C. Full employment surplus analysis and structural change: The 1930s. *Explorations in Economic History*, Winter 1973, 197-210.

Temin, P. *Did monetary forces cause the Great Depression?* New York: Norton, 1976.

Wicker, E. R. Federal Reserve monetary policy, 1922-1933: A reinterpretation. *Journal of Political Economy*, 1965, *LXXIII*, 325-343.

Chapter 2

The Economic Constitution and the New Deal: Lessons for Late Learners

JAMES M. BUCHANAN

The following is an analysis of the Roosevelt New Deal and its consequences in "constitutional" perspective. I interpret the economic legislation of the 1930s and 1940s as changes in the basic "rules of the game," whether or not these changes may be discussed in narrow, legalistic meanings. In effect, the New Deal rewrote the political economic constitution. We are living with the results, and the implications for social order and stability are still emerging. However, we have yet to learn the larger lesson that the New Deal experience should have taught us.

CONSTITUTIONAL FAILURE

Did the pre-New Deal economic constitution of the United States fail? By "economic constitution" I mean the rules of the game, or the constitution, the set of generally expected working properties of institutions of the economic-political order. This constitution was best described in minimal-state, *laissez faire* terms before the New Deal era. The role of the central government was severely circumscribed. This is not to suggest that the motives and ideas in the New Deal were without precursors or that legal and political precedents were wholly absent. The Progressive Era had laid some of the ideational groundwork for New Deal change, and the legal gates had been partially ajar at least since *Munn* v. *Illinois* and, perhaps most important, the Federal Reserve Board had been emplaced with some elements of national monetary coordination.

To some extent I refer to prevailing public attitudes about the economic order. I think that J. R. T. Hughes (1977) had presented convincing evidence that the American attitudes never did embody much positive faith in the working of markets. However, I think that pre-New Deal attitudes about the efficacy of political interference with the economic order were dramatically different from the attitudes that followed. The governmental habit, according to Hughes, was one of piecemeal, pragmatic restriction. The price of milk might be legislated by New York, there being no prevailing public philosophy that said that it should not be, but this was not the same as, nor was it conceived to be the same as, an attempt to coordinate milk pricing and milk marketing nationwide, much less to coordinate the pricing and allocative structure of the existing economy. The latter action was simply not dreamt of in existing public philosophy, again excepting the establishment of the Federal Reserve Board. The economic constitution prior to the New Deal was described as being *laissez faire* in the literal sense; it was not *laissez faire* in its publicly conceived philosophical foundations. Markets were expected to coordinate activities across sectors and regions, because a governmental role in such activity was inconceivable.

In retrospect, we may view the New Deal as having made such a governmental role conceivable to public consciousness. However, this does not suggest that there was a positive motivation for the political coordination of the economy. When we ask, first, why the New Deal made forays beyond the pale previously defined, and, second, why it was at least partially successful in securing acceptability in the public mind, we must look to the negative side of motivation—the almost complete absence of alternatives.

Considered in toto, the economic constitution of the 1920s failed with the Great Depression; coordination broke down. The system did not deliver, and it was seen not to deliver. Normal expectations were not met. The New Deal moved in by default. In the setting of the Great Depression, and without a prevailing public philosophy or understanding of the relative successes and failures of the system's several parts, is there really much surprise that, like a wounded animal, the body politic should have launched out into ill-conceived, mutually contradictory, and self-defeating policies? The economic policies of the New Deal were simplistic in the extreme, and were naively conceived. In short, they were confused reactions to particular institutional circumstances when there seemed to be urgent need for corrective action. Prices had fallen—so why not try to raise prices by legislative-administrative fiat? Men were unemployed—so why not introduce work-sharing schemes? What harm could be done by setting floors on wages and restricting hours? Why not plow under all the little pigs that were in surplus? Since employers did not provide jobs, why not give unions more power? The coal industry was in trouble—so why not cartelize the structure and encourage industry-wide unionization of its labor force? If the price level was tied to gold, why not devalue and improve everything? If full employment was desired, why not have the government guarantee it?

As the aforementioned questions suggest, the New Deal policy responses made up a motley set. In part, they reflected positive reactions to pressures from special interests. In part, they reflected the legislative versions of wild-eyed professors' dreams. In part, they represented the best intentions of legislators who had neither the time nor the competence to examine their long-range consequences. The absence of effectively presented alternatives was perhaps the characteristic feature of all New Deal policy.

There was no sense or understanding of the vital distinction between the constitutional framework of an economy and the operation of the interdependent markets within this constitutional framework. We now know, in retrospect, that a modicum of discrimination would have led to the diagnosis that *only* the monetary elements in the economic constitution had somehow failed and that these elements should have been the direct target for improvement and change.

But this was not to be. In the absence of an offsetting public philosophy and relying on the governmental habit of piecemeal interference with markets, the New Deal placed on the governmental–political structure tasks that it should never have been expected to perform. The failures of the administrative bureaucracy were not, however, to be recognized for decades; and moreover there was widespread conversion to the socialist-inspired doctrine that governments know best, and can solve all problems. Arms and agencies of the central government proliferated, and Washington became the American capital city. In all of this, it is perhaps not surprising that, along with the confusion, some genuinely constitutional improvements were made, some changes in the rules of the game that proved to produce greater stability and efficiency.

WHAT MIGHT HAVE BEEN

It is indeed interesting for us to speculate on the half-century of history that might have taken place if the distinction between the organizational–constitutional framework and the operation of markets within such framework could have been clearly conceived and if policy could have been based on such a conception. What might have been accomplished? What permanent damages to our social fabric might have been avoided? Suppose that the political leaders of the early 1930s, Hoover and/or Roosevelt along with their advisers and the leading members of Congress, could have recognized early that the monetary framework was in shambles. Suppose they could have seen that the breakdown in the American economy could be traced directly to the failures of the fractional reserve banking system interlinked with a national monetary standard tied to gold reserves and with powers of interference resting with the Federal Reserve Board. Suppose that the system's extreme vulnerability to waves of contraction and expansion could have been identified, along with the accompanying recognition that the Federal Reserve authorities were empowered to act without knowledge of what they were about. Suppose that, upon such diagnosis, action could have been taken, early in the 1930s, to sweep away the residues of monetary disaster and to start afresh with a genuinely new "monetary constitution." Suppose that United States currency issue could have been wholly and finally divorced from gold with the limits of fiat issue defined either by a monetary growth rule or by some linkage to a price index. Along with these changes, suppose that 100% reserve banking could have been introduced. It boggles the mind to think what might have been, especially if we assume that the political leaders could have possessed the wisdom that would have allowed them to shun multifarious political interferences with the market process.

Aside from the latter constraint, we may be surprised when we look at the record to see how close we might have been to the enactment of basic components of genuinely permanent reform in the monetary constitution. We know that there were some economists, notably Irving Fisher as well as several members of the University of Chicago group, who were, at the time, calling for monetary-policy reform along the lines sketched. However, these ideas were also in the forefront of discussion and action in the Congress, and, in the almost-anything-goes atmosphere that must have been characteristic of those exciting days, it might have been only an accident that prevented our getting more effective revision in our economic constitution. Robert Weintraub's (1977) recent paper on Wright Patman is of great interest in providing historical detail. Citation at some length is warranted here, both for the intrinsic value of the factual record and for the support that this record lends to my argument that New Deal policy emerged from confused blundering rather than from rational action by political men or from some quasi-mysterious, efficient, institutional response to historical events.

> During the early 1930s, Congress worked its will on a number of bills providing for the issue of additional currency by open market and other operations in such amount as was necessary to increase the index of wholesale prices *back* to the 1921-29 (or, alternatively, the 1926) average, and thereafter to control the issue of currency (sometimes the reference was to currency plus check deposits) so as to stablize the index at that level.... [The Goldsborough] bill declared it "the policy of the United States that the average purchasing power of the dollar as ascertained by the Department of

Labor in the wholesale commodity markets for the period covering the years 1921 to 1929 inclusive, shall be restored and maintained by the control of the volume of credit and currency."

The House passed the Goldsborough bill by a vote of 289 to 60 on May 2, 1932, Mr. Patman voting aye. The bill was killed by the Banking Committee of the Senate. It was vigorously opposed by the Hoover Administration and the Federal Reserve. Fed witnesses (Mayer and Miller) questioned the validity of indexing prices and denied the Fed had powers to fix and stabilize (even approximately) the purchasing power of money. Carter Glass, now a Senator, played the crucial legislative role killing the Goldsborough bill. Goldsborough was scathing in his denunciation of Glass. Addressing the House on June 8 after his bill had been killed, he said, "Some 10 days ago the distinguished Senator from Virginia stated on the floor of the Senate that he would not be willing to give the power provided in this bill to any seven men that God ever made. Does not the Senator from Virginia know that the Federal Reserve System is now exercising these vast powers in an absolutely uncontrolled manner, and does he not know that this legislation would be a limitation upon their powers and their discretion?"

Wright Patman introduced a stable money bill on June 4, 1934. His bill called for redeeming Federal Reserve notes and all other outstanding currency with Treasury notes (greenbacks) and issuing the new currency "in payment of the ordinary expenses of the Federal Government" until there is substantially full employment at the wage and price levels of 1926, and thereafter restricting issue to "a rate not to exceed four percentum per annum." In addition, commercial banks would be required to keep 100 percent reserves in Federal Reserve banks behind demand deposits (and 5 percent behind other deposits) and under the direction of a new Federal Monetary Authority. Federal Reserve banks were to buy and sell securities . . . if the wholesale index fell or rose by 5 percent above or below the 1926 level.

That bill never got off the ground. The Patman (Bonus) bill did. It was an end run that almost succeeded in incorporating variants of the two main principles of the stable money movement of the 1930s into law. First, it provided for reflation. The Treasury would be required . . . to pay for the Adjusted Service Certificates, by having engraved and printed new noninterest-bearing, tax-exempt legal tender Treasury notes; i.e., greenbacks. Second the Patman (Bonus) bill provided for contracting Federal Reserve notes upon a finding by the Secretary of the Treasury that it was necessary to do so to maintain the index of wholesale prices at the 1921-29 level. His bill did not, however, provide for any subsequent currency expansion "beyond implementing the bonus." It was focused on current problems and fears.

The bill passed the House on March 22, 1935, and the Senate on May 7. President Roosevelt vetoed it on May 22. The House overrode the veto the same day by a vote of 324 to 98 against. However, the president's veto was sustained by the Senate the next day, 54 voting for overriding but a 2/3 vote being necessary to override [Robert E. Weintraub. Some neglected monetary contributions: Congressman Wright Patman (1893-1976). *Journal of Money, Credit, and Banking* (November 1977), 520-521].

WHAT WAS

What might have been, indeed. But, out of the lashing about, there did emerge a basic change in the monetary constitution, one that has survived the tests both of time and of critical evaluation. Although it did not seize the day and create a full-reserve banking structure, the Congress, in 1933, went for the next-best option and introduced governmental insurance of bank deposits. As it has turned out, the results have not been too different from those that might have been generated under the 100% reserve system, although, characteristically, more bureaucratic supervision and control necessarily accompanies the insurance scheme. Deposit insurance has modified the economic history of the half century more than many other measures, and it stands in an extremely confined set of institutional changes that must be adjudged to have proved beneficial.

Aside from this single measure, however, the crisis-generated opportunity to reform the monetary constitution constructively was muffed, and the emergence of the Keynesian theory, in 1936, simultaneously distracted attention away from monetary institutions and laid the foundations for the gradual destruction of an important part of the fiscal constitution, the rule of budget balance. Economists were reasonably quick to support fiscal policy, which in practice meant deficit spending, and to give it a predominant role in demand management. The politicians were slow learners, but ultimately they were converted to an economics that played directly to their natural proclivities. Economists remained blithely unaware of the implications of their teachings concerning the constraining rule of budget balance, with consequences that are now available for all to see.[1] As with so many of depression-inspired changes in the basic economic constitution, however, these consequences would not emerge full blown for decades.

The opportunity to amend the nation's monetary constitution faded into limbo after 1936, and the elementary confusion between constitutional structure and the system operating within that structure continued to characterize public and political reality. At this point, my critics may appropriately ask "But was not macroecomics born in 1936, and is this not precisely the sort of distinction that you emphasize?" There are both similarities and differences between the constitutional-operational distinction that I stress and the more familiar distinction of post-Keynesian macroeconomics-microeconomics. Some comparative discussion is warranted, and it may be argued that the Keynesian impact was to add to the confusion rather than to the enlightenment. In my own conception, a constitutional rule defines a process or structure within which certain results, sometimes referred to as end states, emerge from the behavioral interaction of many persons, each one of whom acts independently, subject to the constraints that he privately confronts. Consider the example that was discussed by the Congress in the early New Deal period, a proposal that would direct a monetary authority to stabilize the general price level. This proposal qualifies as a constitutional rule because it establishes the absolute price level as a predictable component of an economy within which the allocation of resources and the setting of

---

[1] For an elaboration of the history and an analysis, see James M. Buchanan and Richard E. Wagner (1977).

2. The Economic Constitution and the New Deal: Lessons for Late Learners

relative prices emerge from the independent actions of many decision makers interacting in many interrelated markets. In one sense, we may say that stability in the absolute price level is an end-state characteristic, desirable in itself. However, in the larger sense, and relevant to my argument, this price-level stability is a *facilitative condition* for the effective functioning of the economy, a functioning that allows the specifically desired results to be generated. Such a rule may be compared and contrasted with the full-employment objective that emerged directly from Keynesian economics and that found its political embodiment in the Full Employment Act of 1946, an act that must be included in any comprehensive catalog of New Deal policy.

Full employment is in itself a highly desirable end state, and its attribute as an end state dominates any facilitative role that its achievement might otherwise play in the functioning of the economy. The desired end state, full employment, *should* emerge from the operation of the market process, provided that the constitutional framework which constrains this process is correctly designed and implemented. However, to direct governmental policy instrumentally toward the attainment of the full-employment end state is necessarily to distract attention from the facilitative conditions that might be required to generate the same result. If the government may instrumentally legislate full employment, what logical consistency remains in an argument that government should not legislate particularized end states for resource use, for prices, for income shares, for rates of growth, for regional economic performance, and for urban and rural development? The post-Keynesian policy emphasis on the employment objective seemed congenial to the natural proclivities of the American politicians to restrict markets pragmatically, and its effects were largely to expand both the public and the political willingness to interfere on increasingly grandiose scales. The post-New Deal conventional wisdom essentially reversed the standing orders of American politics. "Don't just stand there, do something" emerged to characterize both New Deal and post-New Deal political history. The public's measure of political progress came to be discussed in terms of the number of bills passed by the Congress rather than the opposite, and, even in skeptical 1978, the absurd implications of this legislative-quantity criterion seem hardly to be recognized.

I shall not trace in detail the history of post-New Deal follies that were inspired by the threshold piercing patterns of the early federal interventions of the 1930s and 1940s. While Eisenhower slumbered with us through the 1950s, the bureaucratic empire expanded, agencies matured, and attitudes ossified. Few recognized that these were but the cocoon stages for the New Frontier–Great Society activism, surely the apogee for all those who dared to dream of a federally orchestrated and controlled national economy. However, the politicians had finally learned that Keynesian economics had made them free; they could spend without either taxation or guilt. Economists played fine tunes as inflation's fires began to kindle. Johnson's Great Society program was a blunderbuss attempt to implement the New Deal promises that were never intended to move beyond politicians' rhetoric. The transfer society emerged to pass a critical inflection point around 1965.

Environmentalism moved in to capture the romantic fancy of those for whom the New Deal promises had become stale. The established bureaucracy was ready to oblige; regulatory agencies again proliferated, with the costs largely left out of any decision calculus. The arrogant presumption that there is such a thing as free air dominated discussion.

WHAT IS

So much for a selected and personalized sketch of the American history of earlier times. It is now appropriate to freeze the lens and to examine critically the situation that we confront in 1978. I shall discuss only three features: (*a*) the bureaucratic paradox, (*b*) the institutional lock-in, and (*c*) monetary-fiscal disarray.

The Bureaucratic Paradox

Federal benevolence, the predominant image from the 1930s through the 1960s, became federal bureaucracy in the 1970s, with the implication that words in the public philosophy do have meaning. In this respect, the New Deal attitudinal syndrome has disappeared; the faith has gone.[2] Was not the January 1978 funeral celebration for Hubert Humphrey the final acknowledgment that the New Deal flame was not eternal?

We now live with an absence of public confidence in politicians and bureaucrats along with the absence of belief that political-bureaucratic institutions can accomplish results that are either desired or intended. This loss of public confidence in government is solidly grounded. At the level of ordinary observation, political institutions seem to have failed. This perception is supported by sophisticated empirical test results. Accompanying this empirical assessment of the record, there has been the growing acceptance of a theory of political and bureaucratic process that allows us to predict results closely resembling those that we can directly observe.[3] The romantic image of politics as the pure pursuit of public interest has been shattered, perhaps beyond repair.

A paradox arises when we observe the continuing proliferation of federal reg-

---

[2] This shift in public attitudes is acknowledged and discussed from a perspective quite different from my own in Henry J. Aaron (1978).

[3] The theory of public choice can be interpreted in this sense of a "theory of governmental failure" akin to the "theory of market failure" that described the theoretical welfare economics of the 1930s through the 1950s.

ulatory bureaucracy simultaneously with the shift in public attitudes toward it. New and expanded tasks are assigned to politics and to administrative bureaucracy while, at the same time and at other levels of consideration, there is little or no expectation that these tasks will be, or possibly could be, accomplished satisfactorily. How do we explain this?[4]

Three separate explanations may be advanced. Each is partially correct, but, in my view, the first two are subsidiary in relevance to the third. First, the pattern of events does seem to support those who say that government acts and expands its range of controls quite independently of the desires of the citizenry. The observed increase in the size and scope of the political sector may be due to the internal dynamics of a bureaucracy that has attained a life force of its own, subject only to some ultimate threshold constraints imposed by its ability to squeeze resources from the productive elements in the economy. In such a vision of our world, there is really no paradox to be explained.

In a second view, as in the first, there is no anomaly in the results that we observe. The so-called paradox emerges only when we try to impose a unified order on what must be a very complex set of collective-choice institutions. In this second model, unlike the first, there is no independently acting government at all. There is only a complex and interrelated set of institutions, constrained by intricate rules and standing orders. Out of this structure, results emerge that may embody little or no internal coherence, either from the viewpoint of the citizenry or of the bureaucracy itself. It is, therefore, not surprising that some extensions of regulatory control occur simultaneously with other thrusts toward deregulation. It is not a source of wonder that political leaders espouse constraints on the dominance of federal government while actively promoting increasing federal intrusion into economic activity.

As was suggested, there is surely explanatory power in each of these alternative models of modern governmental process. My emphasis here, however, is on a third explanation or model, one in which the "paradox" terminology takes on a more acceptable meaning. We observe a continuing expansion of the political-governmental-collective sector of the economy at the expense of the private-market-individual sector. We recognize the presence of an increasing public consciousness of political-governmental failure because today, as in the 1930s, there is simply no positive public philosophy that contains a nongovernmental alternative. As contrasted with the first explanation above, the third model does allow generalized public preferences to be met via political-bureaucratic institutions, at least in broad directional terms. Further, as contrasted with the second model, the outcomes predicted need not be internally inconsistent. In the third model, however, the coherence of outcomes critically depends on the presence of an integrating philosophy of social order. One of the central themes of this chapter is that the United States has lacked such a philosophy for at least a cen-

[4] For a treatment that parallels this discussion in some respects, see Buchanan (1975).

tury. The crisis atmosphere of the Great Depression allowed for a basic revision of the economic constitution, but this revision was scarcely conscious, and its occurrence was sensed only by members of a Supreme Court who were made to seem mental fossils by the onrush of events. The constitutional revolution of the New Deal was implicit, and, because it was so, the results were not coherent. The New Deal amounted to revolution by default.

The dreams of the New Deal-New Frontier-Great Society have faded because, in a real sense, there was no system to those dreams. The pragmatic patchwork has clearly failed. We find ourselves in a situation somewhat analogous to that of the early 1930s, but there is no crisis, at least not yet, and constitutional revolution does not seem likely to occur by default again. In the 1930s, the system had failed, and, in emergency, we turned to untested, untried, socialist-inspired alternatives, as packaged pragmatically by New Deal advocates. In the 1970s and 1980s, by contrast, there is no untested option that commands more than minimal public support. There is no "Old Deal" waiting in the wings, a movement that might sweep away the political-bureaucratic maze created by a half century of history. Those persons who see hope in the current thrust toward deregulation should look at results, not at rhetoric. Surely the energy policy of 1978 reflects the paradox in unalloyed form. There is little or no public understanding of or faith in the ability of the market process, which offers the only alternative to bureaucracy. Politically, we struggle to choose between two institutional forms, neither one of which commands public respect or engenders public confidence.

The Institutional Lock-In

It is much easier to explain why political-bureaucratic structures, once created, are unlikely to be dismantled than it is to explain why new empires are started. Once a governmental program is instituted, a specific clientele is born, with clearly defined interests in both the maintenance and the expansion of the program's benefits. These interests make themselves felt politically, with the familiar concentration of pressures toward expansion as opposed to the dissipated opposition reflected in the generality of the taxes used to finance the benefits. Even if the structure of a program is widely acknowledged as producing undesired results, it may prove politically impossible to work out the set of compromises and compensations that would be required either to replace or to reform the program in accordance with the promotion of shared objectives.

The OASI (Social Security) program offers the single example worthy of brief discussion. The Roosevelt New Deal was the political vehicle for this Bismarkian transplant onto hitherto alien American ground. Initially, all was promise; little was delivered. The pie was in the sky in the 1930s, but even future pies require resource commitments, and the initial notion was that there would be gradual accumulation of tax-financed fund reserves to meet future benefit commitments. But who could have been so naive as to expect elected politicians in a democracy to tax the citizenry in the absence of currently observed benefits? The 1939 changes in the legislation were telegraphed from the start. The system became an unfunded, pay-as-we-go transfer mechanism, shifting funds from currently productive taxpayers–wage earners to currently retired beneficiaries. However, so long as the labor force was expanding rapidly relative to those who were made eligible for benefits, the tax-transfer costs seemed negligible, and pie remained in the sky for most of those who paid the taxes. New benefits were added, at little apparent political cost and with great political payoffs, and Social Security was, for decades, acclaimed as one of the New Deal's shining monuments.

What happened? In 1978, it is difficult to find articulate, informed defenders of the massive tax-transfer system that currently exists. Almost everyone will say, "How nice it might have been had it been differently organized." The tax-transfer mechanism now in place is widely acknowledged to have a major adverse impact on the rate of productivity growth in the American economy, both from its direct effect on labor inputs and its indirect effect on capital formation. Claims against the system represent the most important item in national wealth in behavioristic terms, yet there is no real stock of wealth existent to meet such claims. To dismantle the system would amount to disavowing these claims; to continue the system amounts to sapping the nation's productive potential. Through time, the tax-transfer system will force American workers to transfer more of their incomes to the provision of retirement stipends than their own preferences would dictate. Conceptually, reform should be possible that would embody compensations such that all persons might be made better off than they are under the current system. However, such reform may be impossible to implement politically.[5]

Monetary-Fiscal Disarray

Earlier I noted that the 1930s were characterized by an absence of any understanding of the distinction between the constitutional structure of an economy and the operation of the related markets within that structure. It would, indeed, be satisfying if I could, at this point, assert that intellectual progress has been great, that such an understanding has now become much more widespread. Such an assertion would reflect wishful thinking rather than reality. We need only look to the 1978 public, political, and academic discussion of employment and inflation to see that the confusion is almost as prevalent now as it was then.

Keynesian economics effectively destroyed an important part of the previously existing fiscal constitution: the rule of budget balance. This rule, which was

---

[5] For a discussion of the problems here, see Buchanan (1977).

interpreted to be a constraint on budgets except during emergencies, forced decision makers to measure the opportunity costs of governmental spending programs with reasonable accuracy. In the absence of this rule, these costs are lowered; spending programs seem less costly than they are. Government spending expands disproportionately. Deficits have become permanent and are accelerating in size with time. Politically, however, it has become impossible to achieve a regime of budget balance regardless of the macroeconomic setting.

Even this obvious flaw in the fiscal-monetary constitution might be contained with little other than a pronounced public-spending bias if there should exist an offsetting monetary constitution, a rule or set of rules that would allow for predictability in the structural macroeconomic setting. However, no such set of rules describes the post-Keynesian economy of the 1970s. Budget deficits place on monetary authorities the conflicting requirements to maintain reasonable stability in interest rates and in the general price level while, at the same time, being charged with concern for both the full employment objective and the position of the dollar in international currency markets. Stagflation has become the observed result, and the developing expectation seems to be that the discretion of the politicians and of the monetary authorities can be counted on only to keep both inflation and unemployment within tolerable bounds, with the acknowledged resource costs that both of these phenomena embody.

IMPLICATIONS FOR REFORM

What are some of the implications of the New Deal experience, considered in its totality, for our time, for potential reform in the 1980s?

Several elements of my answer to this question have been evident in my discussion of recent history. We must learn to make the distinction between the constitutional structure or framework of an economy and the operations of institutions constrained within this framework. We must learn that the market process does present a viable alternative to bureaucratic chaos, provided only that the framework, the laws and institutions, are properly constructed. We must learn, and learn better, the central principle of economic theory, the principle of the spontaneous coordination achieved only by market process. We must learn the simple lessons of public-choice theory, which teach that politics and the political man cannot be predicted to promote some vaguely defined public interest.

We must learn these lessons in order to better design and control the political economy. Economics is not like astronomy, in that the movement of the stars is not within man's powers of control. In economics, we learn to predict how an economy operates under alternative institutional constraints, and these constraints do not evolve naturally in some ineluctable process of history. We learn about them in order to design improvements, and we look to the political-governmental process to implement and to enforce change. We learn economics in order to make better political decisions and in order to use our intelligence to reform the constitutional setting within which we are to operate as economizing agents.

In our blundering efforts as professional economists, we have been far too preoccupied with efficiency as the end state characteristic in the operation of an economy. We have talked about "market failure" and "market success" almost exclusively in efficiency terms. We have said far too little about the political function of market organization, about the liberty of markets, and about the voluntary features of trade that are necessarily removed by the shift to any collective alternative. Democratic politics, too, must be constrained within a constitutional framework, and such politics can function only if their operational tasks are severely limited. The market's primary role is to allow depoliticization of major areas of allocative choice. We have said far too little about the justice of markets," despite the fact that Adam Smith put much stress on this element in his historic book. It is a violation of "the justice of his natural liberty" to restrain the teen-aged black from employment through a minimum-wage law, quite apart from and beyond its effect on efficiency.

If the "we" in my answers here referred only to professional economists, there might be some grounds for cautious optimism. Some solutions are to be found here and there in our literature, and other elements may be found lurking between the lines. But professional economists are not likely to be assigned roles as philosopher kings, and they are equally unlikely to be called upon to give advice to genuinely benevolent despots. The "we" must refer, not to the professional economists, but to the general public, and, in some more inclusive sense, to all those who act in various ways to influence policy and politicians. What should the experience of 50 years have taught us, as professional economists, about the potential for the attainment of wisdom on the part of the public?

To the naive among us, the results might suggest the need for more and better economic education, carrying more or less the content that our curricula now embody, but here we run squarely up against the evidence that modern university economics does not provide the normative understanding that I have called for in the foregoing. Instead, the evidence suggests that such instruction provides no understanding for students that is retained for periods sufficiently long to make the whole exposure relevant. Indeed, perhaps the cynics who offer that the best to be said for instruction in economics is that it is better than instruction in sociology are right, at least in their low opinion of university economics. In any case, let us acknowledge that the elementary textbooks must be rewritten; the courses and curricula redesigned. We must cease our efforts to make students into imaginary social engineers on the one hand or into empty empiricists on the other. It is more important that law and ethics enter economics than it is that economics enter law and ethics.

Nevertheless, we must not be apologetic for our subject matter or demeaning to the normative philosophic position that defines it. We are the keepers and the transmitters of intellectually respectable arguments that defend the structural features of the only societies in history that have been free and prosperous. Without renewed efforts at explicit articulation of this defense, pragmatic and unprincipled politics will generate results desired by no one. If the New Deal and its consequences teach us anything at all, it surely must be that a society lacking a public philosophy must drift toward its own Sargasso Sea.

ACKNOWLEDGMENT

I am indebted to my colleagues, Robert Tollison and Gordon Tullock for helpful suggestions.

REFERENCES

Aaron, H. J. *Politics and the professors.* Washington: Brookings Institution, 1978.
Buchanan, J. M. *The limits of liberty.* Chicago: University of Chicago Press, 1975.
Buchanan, J. M. Comment on Browning's paper. In C. Campbell (Eds.) *Financing Social Security.* Washington: American Enterprise Institute, 1979. Pp. 208-212.
Buchanan, J. M., and Wagner, R. E. *Democracy in deficit: The political legacy of Lord Keynes.* New York: Academic Press, 1977.
Hughes, J. R. T. *The governmental habit.* New York: Basic Books, 1977.
Weintraub, R. E. Some neglected monetary contributions: Congressman Wright Patman (1893-1976). *Journal of Money, Credit, and Banking,* November 1977, 520-521.

Discussion

ROBERT W. CLOWER

As usual, I have profited greatly from reading Professor Buchanan's chapter, partly because I learned from it some things I did not previously know. Much of what he says is in agreement with my own view of the economy of the 1930s and of the state of economics at the present time. That being so, however, it is all the more important that I concentrate in my remarks on my disagreements rather than my agreements with Professor Buchanan, for only by that procedure can I expect to add anything in the way of perspective to what has already been said.

Professor Buchanan has argued that there was a fundamental change in the rules of the game or in the economic constitution of the United States in the 1930s, and that the New Deal and its legislation are to be explained largely in terms of this change. I agree that there were changes in the economic constitution of the United States, but I do not think they took place in the 1930s; on the contrary, I would argue that what happened in the 1930s constituted simply a series of moves within a game whose rules had already been abrogated during the preceding two decades. Some of these departures were related to the experience of "economic planning" that accompanied our entry into World War I.

Other departures were connected with the creation of the Federal Reserve System which, during the 1920s, began to play fast and loose with the rules of the Gold Standard in order to pursue a supposedly rational policy of intervention in the domestic money market. One way and another, most of the machinery that would later be used by the New Deal was already in place before 1929. Contrary to common belief, moreover, not all members of the Supreme Court in the 1920s were averse to using the judicial process to play God with the economic and political system of the United States.

The changes in the rules of the game that occurred before 1929 were not accompanied by major political or economic upheaval because pressures making for change (arising mainly within the intellectual community) were vigorously resisted by powerful and self-confident business interests, but the resistance eroded after the 1929 Crash. In effect, the Federal Reserve System engineered the downturn by not adhering to the rules of the Gold Standard, and then converted what might have been a relatively minor recession into a Great Depression by refusing to break completely with the Gold Standard, as would have been required to "reflate" the economy in 1930 and 1931. The demoralization of the business community that accompanied the subsequent banking crises and the prolongation of the depression effectively eliminated the only serious forces of opposition to radical reorganization of the economic system.

This brings me to another point of disagreement with Professor Buchanan. Professor Buchanan argues that the events of the 1930s might not have occurred had the economics profession been more successful in propagating a philosophy of social order along with its teaching of basic economic principles. In my view, this is almost the reverse of the truth. Indeed, I would argue that the absence in the 1930s of any serious technical discipline that would allow economists to deal intelligently with short-run economic processes left them in a position of having nothing to teach except second-rate sociology and a doctrinaire commitment to the self-adjusting proclivities of the economic system. In these circumstances, economists could not be expected to give intelligent guidance to practical men, or even to madmen in authority, as to how possibly disastrous side effects of economic intervention and regulation might be avoided. By default, economists acted more as preachers than as teachers, for they had nothing useful to teach.

Nor have matters changed all that much since the 1930s. Despite the Keynesian Revolution and its aftermath, we still find ourselves in a position where we are unable to agree among ourselves about the short-run consequences of alternative policies of economic intervention. Now, as in the 1930s, there is a general commitment in the United States to the idea that the vast bulk of goods and services should be produced and distributed in accordance with the dictates of the free market. However, there is also a feeling, now as then, that the free market does not always perform as effectively as might be wished. Intervention is sometimes necessary. Unfortunately, our understanding of the workings of the economic system is still confined largely to generalities about the working of ghostly forces of supply and demand and about the marvelous way in which the price system operates to coordinate the trading, production, and consumption activities of individuals. We do not have a coherent theory of the actual working of markets as institutions that are organized and operated by flesh-and-blood individuals. As a matter of ordinary common sense, it is obvious to most of us that the modern economic system would collapse if one eliminated the millions of middlemen who serve as centers for the transmission of economic messages from households to business firms. But we do not know how breakdowns in the effective coordination of economic activities might be prevented, much less what might then be done by way of government intervention to make the normal message centers of the economy function more effectively. As a consequence, we deal with symptoms of problems rather than origins, and the result is regulations that as often as not exacerbate the very problems they are designed to solve.

I am reminded here of J. M. Keynes's often-quoted observation "How splendid it would be if we economists could some day manage to get ourselves thought of as humble, competent people, on a level with dentists or engineers." Certainly it would be desirable for economists, like dentists, to be able to distinguish between, as it were, cases of economic toothache and cases of economic lockjaw. And I have the feeling that if the economics profession could so distinguish, then in the not-too-distant future the profession might be in a position to speak with one voice about what kinds of economic intervention would and would not promote the effective coordination of economic activities within the free market sector of the economy.

So I conclude by remarking once more that I disagree with Professor Buchanan's view of the proper role of the economics profession. I think we need to direct our attention to the mechanics of market exchange and not to the philosophy of social order. It seems plain enough that we are not going to go back to an earlier era when widespread government intervention in economic affairs was unknown. We are going to have to live with economic regulation. The business of economists, therefore, should be to ensure that such regulations as are adopted perform their intended function and do not have seriously disadvantageous side effects. Our problem now, as in the 1930s, is not only that regulatory change occurs in an atmosphere of crisis but that it continues to take place in an atmosphere of ignorance.

Chapter 3

Roots of Regulation: The New Deal

JONATHAN HUGHES

My task here is to fit the New Deal into the historical perspective of its long-run effects on regulation. This is not easy, because of the breadth of relevant historical factual material, and I must, perforce, reduce both the facts of long-term history and the New Deal into manageable proportions. I begin with a broad view of regulation, broad enough to include the word *influence*, because government was sometimes able to get its way (with subsidies for example) without the necessity of imposing the controlling apparatus of direct regulation.

By now, government influence and regulation have given us an economy of $N - 1$ choice sets. The missing set is the one in which economic agents choose their operating levels strictly on the basis of costs and prices — the decisions that the market alone would prompt. To what extent this result is necessarily inferior, I leave to others. It is a difficult problem. We obviously do not want to abolish government regulation, yet there is no general agreement on where and how much of it we should have. We were developing an extensive network of nonmarket controls at all levels of government long before the New Deal (Hughes, 1977). Each control was satisfactory to some group at some time, but there was no overall rationale, and no electorate was ever given the choice of accepting or rejecting the entire package. The New Deal augmented this process of piecemeal growth of regulation and federalized it to an extent never before known, except temporarily in World War I.

By now the New Deal era ought to be settled in historical perspective. The Japanese ended the Great Depression, and Roosevelt and Hopkins should, by now, be like Tojo and Yamashita—mere historical shades and parts of the great past. A man born in 1933 would, after all, now be 45-years old, possibly a grandfather. Yet the New Deal is still an emotional thing. It is a tribute to the New Deal's impact on the American imagination that it still evokes such emotion and interest. However, discussion of Roosevelt and the New Deal often produces more heat than light, even after 4 decades. Why is this?

Partly, the New Deal was an ideological affront. It was a historical thumbednose at both neoclassical economics and the moral basis for private business's claim to preference as a training camp for leadership in American life beyond the counting house. The Great Depression of the 1930s wrought havoc on both, and they never recovered. Free-market economics and business leaders have been relatively low in public esteem ever since (Krooss, 1970).

But there is something else; the New Deal was a vital inflection point on the upward curve of federal power, and the long-term consequence is something that sticks in our collective throat. Ever since the 1930s, the power of the government in Washington, D.C., has waxed and all other power, private, state, and local government, has diminished accordingly. As Bertrand De Jouvenel (1962) emphasized power is a zero-sum game: There is enough of it in the world to control entirely the lives of all persons, and either it is left with individuals or someone else has it. Since the 1930s, that someone else has been, in over-growing proportions, the federal government.

It now appears that it was not what was done in the 1930s, but where it was done, that mattered. It was not, primarily, the imposition of more nonmarket controls over persons, but the federal assumption of the power to impose them together with its prolific activism in the economy that made the New Deal such a critical change in American history and that qualified it for the word *revolutionary*. The process of federal expansion, which had, for nearly 150 years, been very slow (always receding after wars, for example) now increased in power and magnitude. We never went back to the old balance of power between the states and the federal government, which had characterized the federal system.

If we are to understand the New Deal and its historic mission (whether we like it or not), it is this single phenomenon that we must explain. *How* it was done is not so important as *why*, for it can be shown that virtually all of the New Deal was in principle as American as cherry pie by 1933. However, most of it was not part of the federal government's own history. The roots lay elsewhere deep in the nation's history, in the states and even in the colonies before that.

THE ENTREPRENEURIAL GOVERNMENT FIRM

For the most part, the macroeconomics of the New Deal era captured the imagination of the world and of the economics profession. Both the realities and the potentials of the magical words *fiscal policy* motivated new political alignments, ambitious plans, economic models, and visions of full employment with price stability.[1] Later on, after the Treasury Accord of 1950 ended the Federal Reserve System's Babylonian Captivity, monetary policy came back for a season in new, glamorous raiments. At its peak, in the finely tuned Camelot of the early 1960s, the macroeconomic heritage of the 1930s appeared to augur a bright new future.

However, now we can see that the phenomena that my colleague Louis Cain calls the microeconomics of governmental development in the New Deal had a basic and lasting impact. The governmental "firms"—agencies, commissions, controls, boards, offices, and administrations—"selling" their services (usually monopolistically) to the economic system have lasted, and expanded their scope and size. In terms of budgetary expenditures, agency regulation was not costly, so it attracted only marginal interest. However, these controls change the flow of productive factors if their rulings are observed. They have become, as Murray Weidenbaum (1977) and others (Jansen and Meckling 1977) now emphasize, ubiquitous federal decision making, inserted by law into the private sector. Growing mushroomlike out of the older tradition of police powers, these firms became a solid structure of economic power. Berkowitz and McQuaid (1978) have shown that the aggressive, competitive, and entrepreneurial dimensions of this industry have long been underestimated in the conventional wisdom of scholars.

By the late 1970s, when fiscal policy had become merely an accounting of the annual growth of federal expenditures (along with the supporting taxes, deficits, debt monetization, and inflation), when monetary-policy debates had become media events centered on the personalities of financial luminaries, the industry of federal-agency regulation seemed now to be the cut-in-stone legacy of the New Deal. The microeconomics of firm, product, industry, and activity control may well embrace the preponderance of governmental power to determine the structure of economic activity and its volume in this economy's future. Dramatic changes in governmental macroeconomics seem unlikely. Spending levels must, it would appear, simply rise every year in the future. But what will be

---

[1] Compare, for example, two retrospective views, one near to event and one 3 decades later, Arthur Smithies (1946) and Herbert Stein (1969). Horace M. Gray (1940) thought that the commission form of nonmarket control had spent its force, largely because of its own irrationality. They " . . . all followed the delusion that private privilege can be reconciled with public interest by the alchemy of public regulation" (p. 281).

produced, and how it will be priced, who will or will not invest, what technologies will be deployed, which industries will grow or vanish, how many will be employed and where, in what racial mixtures and at what wages—these are the main elements of governmental microeconomics. Controls of these decisions at the firm level have become lodged in federal agencies.

It is important to understand the basic congeniality of these controls. We wanted them. They are rooted in our history, laws, constitutions, and traditions. Whatever may be debated in the future among economists and political leaders regarding optimal macro-policy proposals, the regulatory legacy of the New Deal seems likely to remain unchallenged. It is too fundamentally a part of the American economy to face extinction or, perhaps, even meaningful reform. Considering the political difficulties in decontrol of natural gas or in finding a policy between controls and noncontrol in the oil industry alone, one can sense the magnitude of our political snarl. These are huge industries with supposedly powerful influence in Washington. What of the thousands of other controls we now have? If we are unable to find solutions to a handful of major regulatory problems, what chance is there to untangle the rest? The regulations are the products of our economic and political history. Each represents a solution, or nonsolution, to a problem, woven into past political and social evolution. We could overturn our own historical legacy by a massive political effort, but that seems an utterly unlikely possibility. We have long found our congeries of nonmarket controls to be congenial, even if there are potent and detailed objections to each mode and technique of control. The New Deal's contribution was to help galvanize all this onto the body of the American economy.

SUBSIDIES AND EXPENDITURES

Let us begin the analysis with the subsidy, a sometimes subtle, yet fruitful source of regulatory power. Actually, the economic difference between a subsidy and a direct control is minimal. The outcome is essentially the same: The economy renders some result it would not have without the subsidy (or control) and, if the subsidy creates net income redistribution, the economy also lacks something it otherwise could have had. To see the history of regulation in this country, we need to consider subsidies as a form of regulation, and the New Deal was an important part of that history. The New Deal somehow managed to identify itself with subsidies in the 1930s and, temporarily, to do for the subsidy what Vietnam did for war—give it a bad name. Plowing under the little pigs, leaf-raking, and PWA boondoggles were the media events associated with New Deal subsidy programs, and they were given spectacular publicity by the opposition press. Perhaps such public exposures of subsidies were new, but there are few things in the government policy toolbox more honored by time and usage than the subsidy. From time out of mind, governments have subsidized activities to get things done that the market seemed not to favor: to establish, locate, and encourage enterprises that policymakers desired.

In our case, Clair Wilcox (1960) did not exaggerate when he wrote, "Government has subsidized private enterprise, both in industry and in agriculture, throughout the nation's history. Exemptions from royal taxation in the earliest colonial enterprises were one subsidy technique of the Crown to encourage settlement (Thorpe, 1909). Harvard College was granted 400 pounds in 1636 together with the revenues from the Charleston-Boston ferry (itself a special franchise monopoly). In 1659, a further 100 pounds were granted by the Massachusetts government, "to be payd by the Treasurer of the Country to the Colledg Treasurer. for the behoof and maintenance of the President and Fellows" (Whitmore, 1889).

Colonial history is filled with direct and indirect subsidies granted to encourage trade, the building of wharfs, and agriculture (mulberry trees and silk worms). In Federal America, direct subsidy, together with monopoly grants by states, was a favored technique. The federal government's role in these enterprises was mainly a minor one, although later on, with the railroad land grants, it became more visible (Goodrich, 1960). The first tariff act of Congress, July 4, 1789, (USPGO, 1896) was explicitly protective:

> Whereas it is necessary for the support of the government, for the discharge of the debts of the United States, and the encouragement and protection of manufactures, that duties be laid on goods, wares and merchandise imported . . . [p. 9].

Defense contracts were standard sources of subsidies to manufacturers from the beginning; Eli Whitney's musket contract of 1789 was something like a modern book contract with a $5000 advance and, with royalties, a total payment of $134,000. As Whitney said: "By this contract, I obtained some thousands of dollars in advance which has saved me from ruin" (Hughes, 1973). The states commonly made grants and loans to establish manufacturing in the antebellum period, just as municipalities now offer property tax relief to attract industry (Goodrich, 1967). The two big silver purchase acts of the late 19th century were major subsidizations of that industry, and, of course, another was achieved in the Silver Purchase Act of 1934.

When is a government purchase not a subsidy? Presumably when the seller has one or more alternatives and the opportunity cost of selling to the government is not negative; more generally, if the seller collects no rents or quasi-rents from the government purchase. But what of government purchases that create new activities? There are no alternative buyers. Many of the New Deal purchases from the private sector came in new programs: learning-by-doing in the realm of spending. This was one of their legacies to us: how to spend federal funds without war. Those who know the period's history will recall how the sheer problem

TABLE 3.1
Construction Expenditures on Federal Public Works

(Mean annual proportions in percentage of totals fiscal years)

	Harding	Coolidge	Hoover	R. I	R. II	R. III (1941 only)
Defense	22.5	9.0	12.1	10.0	15.3	58.6
Rivers and harbors	43.3	54.6	22.7	24.8	18.1	2.9
Water use and control	4.4	10.8	16.9	23.5	34.8	18.4
Public buildings	3.8	4.3	23.7	22.0	12.5	3.7
All other	26.0	21.3	24.6	19.7	19.3	16.4
Total	100.0	100.0	100.0	100.0	100.0	100.0
Average annual expenditures ($ millions)	134.8	118.6	249.8	399.6	553.6	1,533.8

Source: National Resources Planning Board, *Development of resources and stabilization of employment in the United States*: Part I, *The federal program for national development*. Washington, D.C.: U.S. Government Printing Office, 1941. Calculated from Table 1, p. 82.

of spending vexed the early New Dealers.[2] Only Harry Hopkins, at first, seemed able to inject money quickly into the economy in large amounts (Sherwood, 1950). The others had to plan and make programs. But which plans, which programs? Table 3.1 serves to illustrate, very roughly, the progress of these developments between the wars. The data are for federal construction expenditures on federal projects alone.

As expenditures increased, new absorption areas had to be found. Hoover doubled Coolidge's expenditures on public works. Roosevelt I was 60% above Hoover; Roosevelt II was 30% above Roosevelt I and 120% above Hoover. Ignoring defense expenditures, one sees the vital role played by "rivers and harbors"—the sum of Congressional wisdom—which were roughly half of the total expenditures in the Harding and Coolidge years. But of course, rivers and harbors could not have devoured half of the expenditures of Roosevelt II. New ideas were needed. Hoover, when the heat was on, built new public buildings and entered (via irrigation projects) into water use and control. By Roosevelt II, this category alone was able to absorb nearly 35% of federal construction expenditures (again, on federal projects), an amount greater than Harding or Coolidge ever spent in total on federal public works. Consider Hoover in 1932 compared with Roosevelt in 1939. These data are *total* federal expenditures including grants, loans, guarantees, and federal-corporation expenditures.

[2] For an interesting primer on how to do it, see The National Planning Board's *Criteria and planning for public works,* written by a private consultant, Russell V. Black, and distributed by the Federal Emergency Administration of Public Works in 1934. It was published as a reproduced typescript. I am indebted to my colleague, R. B. Heflebower, for introducing me to this fascinating document.

TABLE 3.2
Water Use and Control ($ millions)*

Fiscal years	Flood control	TVA	Reclamation and irrigation	Transmission and electric power	Public water systems	Public sewerage	Miscellaneous
1932 total $51.6 million	28.0	—	23.6	.02	—	—	—
1939 total $488.9 million	76.4	31.5	129.2	24.3	85.6	138.7	2.7

*Source: See source cited for Table 3.1, Calculated from Table 6, p. 100.

One finds such originality throughout the federal tables of expenditures and employment (in national parks, forests, and soil conservation, for example). The increasing amounts spent depended upon the discovery of new ways to spend—such being necessary until war came again and a vast increase in military expenditures finally reduced the depression levels of unemployment. The New Deal budgets were, by our modern standards, inconsiderable. However, they were, in the wages and prices of the interwar period, big increases over the previous decade. Roosevelt-I expenditures (averaging $6.6 billions) exceeded Hoover's average expenditures by 78%, and Roosevelt II was above the Hoover administration by 118%. All of that occurred within less than a decade, after all, with federal permanent civilian employment rising nearly 60% in just 7 years.[3] Concerning federal construction, the New Deal expansion was deemed triply necessary since it substituted for the substantial collapse of the private, state-government and local-government sectors. They never regained the levels of the 1920s throughout the New Deal years, despite the subsidies and aids granted them by the federal government (National Resources Planning Board, 1940).

It will be useful to give two specific examples of the purpose of the Federal subsidy: (*a*) to appropriate power from persons and (*b*) to take power from lower levels of government. The first case is revealed in agriculture and the second by rivers and harbors, and water transport.

Agriculture was in a disastrous condition in the 1930s. Farmers had been agitating for federal assistance since the 1880s. The New Deal mobilized Congressional votes to bring many old programs into law. For example, the establishment of the Export-Import Bank in 1934 (reorganized in 1936) helped to meet a long-standing demand, voiced in the McNary-Haugen bills of the 1920s, that surplus be disposed of in foreign markets. Coolidge vetoed McNary-Haugen bills twice; Hoover picked up the ball with the Agricultural Market Act and the Federal Farm Board in 1929. By lending money ($500 millions) to farm co-ops and stabilization corporations, it was hoped that farm incomes could be bolstered. By 1930, the Farm Board held a third of the nation's wheat supply (Fausold, 1977).

Roosevelt's advisers went far beyond that in their efforts to aid agriculture. They tried production control, soil conservation, price supports, and parity payments. No doubt the best-known legacy of this period was the Commodity Credit Corporation (1933), which lent money against stored crops, thus realizing in essence the subtreasury scheme of the Populists (Hughes, 1977). Subsidies to agriculture in 1932-1939 were estimated at 3.8 billion dollars (Joint Economic Committee, 1960). The supplemental Agricultural Marketing Agreement Act, of

---

[3] *Historical statistics of the United States,* United States Government Printing Office, Washington, D.C., 1960. Table Y 254–257 on budget expenditures; Y 241–250 on paid civilian employment. In Washington, D.C., 73,455 in 1932, 129,314 in 1939; elsewhere, 532,041 in 1932 and 824,577 in 1939.

1938, fixed the prices paid to producers of milk and fruit and also relieved their cooperative organizations of the weight of the antitrust acts. Here again, the combination of subsidy and regulations proved a potent and long-term force, but relief from antitrust prosecution was nothing more than had existed in some cases for other regulated industries almost since the inception of the antitrust laws (Liebhafsky, 1971; Simpson, 1929-1930). The Federal Farm Loan Act, of 1916, had realized another Populist demand, that agricultural land be more easily mortgagable than it had been since 1892 under the dominance of the National Banking System (which the Populists wanted abolished outright) (Hicks, 1961; see also the platforms of the Southern Alliance and Knights of Labor, and of the Northern Alliance). A propensity in subsidizing and controlling agriculture had, of course, been encouraged by the command economy of World War I, when the Lever Food Control Act (1917) was used to achieve price supports together with quantitative controls (Hughes, 1977). By the end of the 1930s, farmers were assisted on a scale they had never known before; they also were well enmeshed in the system of federal controls that have since characterized the farm sector. A similar New Deal recrudescence of wartime experience was the Federal Housing Administration (backed by the RFC Mortgage Company and the Federal National Mortgage Association). It was in part a rebirth of the United States Housing Corporation, of World War I, which actually built houses and put defense workers into them. The Reconstruction Finance Corporation was itself, of course, the old War Finance Corporation (1918) in new clothes, but it had been called back into life by Hoover, not Roosevelt.

In the case of water transport, improvement of rivers and harbors, and aids to operation, we have a case of federal assumption of powers that were developed earlier by state and local governments. Subsidies of inland waterways and harbors, traditional pork-barrel items and sturdy bulwarks of federal spending, have a long history, although, in absolute amounts, the New Deal spending efforts here were dramatic. Between 1912 and 1936, some $2.9 billions had been spent on rivers and harbors, but a third of that amount was spent in 1933-36 alone (Liebhafsky, 1971).

Government involvement in water transport goes back to earliest colonial times. It is difficult to see how private individuals could profitably dredge major public channels and harbors—a good example of private costs far exceeding any conceivable private gain. This was well understood at the beginning. In Federal America, the Gallatin Plan embodied a comprehensive system of such expenditures, but the Federal government did not act. As Goodrich and others have shown, mainly state- and local-government subsidies achieved what Gallatin wanted, together with expenditures by private-business interests (Goodrich, 1957; Hill, 1957; Haitus, Mak, and Walton, 1975). So, at first, failure at the federal level resulted in state action and a concomitant increase of state power. Federal involvement, although proportionately small, did traditionally include the services of the Army engineers, an involvement that would play a crucial role in the future of rivers-and-harbors expenditures.

The modern system of Army-engineer control of expenditures can be traced directly to the Rivers and Harbors Act, of 1902. Expanded federal responsibility was the purpose of Theodore Roosevelt's Inland Waterways Commission, of 1907. Its work was continued by the National Waterways Commission, of 1909, which advocated in 1912 comprehensive federal engineering, planning, and subsidies to integrate water and rail transport. During World War I, these targets were partly realized by both subsidy and direct federal development and operation of transport equipment. In 1920, the residual government barge lines on the Mississippi and Warrior rivers were turned over to the War Department for continued operation. In 1929, the Inland Waterways Corporation was established with full federal stock ownership to operate the line. This corporation was finally placed within the Commerce Department by legislation in 1939 (Locklin, 1947). By then, the modern edifice of federal control over waterways had come into existence.

Since the waterways are "highways," the government has the unquestioned power to monitor passage and set tolls. As was true of so much of the federal expansion of power in the 1930s, it was the "commerce-clause revolution" that paved the way. Indeed, there is an air of inevitability in this history. In *Oklahoma* v. *Atkinson*, in 1941, the rule for ubiquitous control of waters was set out: "[C]ongress may exercise its control over the nonnavigable stretches of a river in order to preserve and promote commerce on the navigable portions. Water carriers with rail links were under the regulation of the ICC according to the Interstate Commerce Act of 1887, and by 1909 this had become a settled matter in law. The Panama Canal Act of 1912 gave the ICC control over rail-owned water carriers. The federal government became, as part of its rate-control powers, a sponsor of price-fixing maritime cartels—conference rates—under the Shipping Act of 1916. The resulting Federal Shipping Board operated until 1936, when it was reorganized as the National Maritime Commission, with extensive regulatory powers, expanded to coastal shipping by the Intercoastal Shipping Act of 1938 (Joint Economic Committee, 1960; Liebhafsky, 1971).

I bring up this piece of history because we see in it a shift from state to federal power as part of the natural development of federal powers under the commerce clause. It is interesting that the failure of the federal government to act in the early years did not mean no government participation, but rather government participation at the state level.

In addition, there is the matter of federal subsidies for construction of ships, operating equipment, and operating costs, which is part of this history, but would require far more space than can be accorded it here. In the New Deal years, the Merchant Marine Acts of 1934 and 1936 reorganized the older subsidy system (going back to the inception of mail subsidies in 1845) and provided a permanent system to subsidize both construction and operating costs (Joint

Economic Committee, 1960; Liebhafsky, 1971). It is obvious, if you consider maritime subsidies, that no state government now could have raised such moneys to finance business firms (Green, 1973). That required federal power.

We could go on at great length: air transport, airport construction, radio communications, education, housing, conservation, highways—the list, while not perhaps endless, may well be beyond the powers of scholarship to complete. Who now could trace the whole list of economic activities subsidized by the federal government? The New Deal made a notable contribution to this tradition. It may well be that the federal involvement, subsidizing everything from sidewalks to giant multi-purpose dams and airports, made great contributions and imposed higher technical standards than we would have obtained otherwise. We see in the New Deal a growing sense of confidence about subsidies, a diminution of defensiveness, and the beginning of the widespread present belief that subsidies are good for everyone. They always were good for those who received the money. The degree of control in a given subsidey varies, but control often seems a small price to pay for the largesse from an N.S.F. research grant or a new steamship or whatever.

FEDERAL ESTABLISHMENT OF UNIONS

Scholars and others are often puzzled by the Wagner Act (1935), the major New Deal intervention in the centuries-old struggle for a mutually satisfactory framework for wage-bargain negotiations. Since the act establishes nodes of monopoly power in the labor force, it seems out of phase with the antimonopoly tradition of common law and the antitrust acts. Federal sponsorship of independent labor power may also seem strange in a supposedly capitalist nation.

The Wagner Act involved not the provision of equity to individuals but recognition of rights of unions in the "corporate property" of labor. Federal power transferred to organized labor an amount of leverage that no collection of unorganized individuals could have had. Federal establishment of unions remains something of a puzzle, because the rights of employers which were so powerful at the country's beginning (including outright ownership of persons in slavery and, of their labor for terms of years, in cases of white servitude), were slowly and relatively peacefully diluted enough to make collective bargaining mandatory where NLRA conditions are met. This outcome confounds ideology. A capitalist state appears an unlikely one to have yielded voluntarily to the demands of its workers, especially when they had no separately organized political power of their own. In the United States, the force of the labor vote could be registered without a separate labor party, and workers need not turn to socialism to achieve collective-bargaining power. As Gompers related, the completely conservative AFL came out of a socialist study group whose ideas about revolutionary change were transmuted into "business unionism" by American reality (Perlman, 1949).

The state was always involved in these issues in Anglo-American history, but given the common-law origins, governments had customarily been on the side of real and intangible property rights in the wage bargain. Traditionally, wages, hours, and working conditions had been set by courts, privileged trade organizations, townships, magistrates, and other official bodies (Hughes, 1976). Even in Federal America, wages were not due workers if they quit before the expiration of their contracts. Yet the courts at that time allowed variations for businesses: For example, builders could recover "off the contract" if work was terminated before completion (Horowitz, 1977). Unions were criminal conspiracies before *Commonwealth* v. *Hunt* (1842), and they faced another 9 decades of mainly adverse court decisions after that.

Nevertheless, there was a persistent tide running in labor's favor, evidenced by such things as the early appearance of mechanic lien laws[4] and continued widespread sentiment in labor's favor. The states wrote legislation outlawing yellow-dog contracts (for example, Indiana, in 1893) (Millis and Montgomery, 1945; Mueller, 1949), and organized labor found allies in political coalitions; for example, the statements of solidarity with labor in the various Populist platforms of 1889-1892.[5] When the Sherman Act was used against labor,[6] there followed the famous disclaimer in the Clayton Act, together with its efforts to limit injunctions against union activity.[7] Such evidence reflects a political reality: There were millions of manual workers, their numbers were growing with industrialization, and their concentration in urban congressional districts made politicians aware of them. Unlike their European counterparts, American workers were full citizens, with the right to vote after property qualifications were removed early in the nineteenth century (Perlman, 1949). Ideas about equity between labor and capital could hardly be suppressed in such circumstances. The use of laws of incorporation to acquire special privileges for capital agglomerations had, by the end of the nineteenth century, produced the characteristically giant enter-

---

[4] Pennsylvania had a mechanic's lien law in 1803. By 1826, Chancellor Kent wrote that such laws were generally in force in the United States (James Kent, 1884).

[5] Hicks, Populist platforms: St. Louis (1890), p. 427; Northern Alliance (1891) p. 430, Cincinnati (1891) p. 435, St. Louis (1892) pp. 435-439, Omaha (1892) pp. 439-444.

[6] *Loewe* v. *Lawlor*, 208 U.S. 274 (1908). In 1894, Attorney General Olney had invoked the Sherman Act as a weapon against the Pullman strikers in Illinois, and Debs had been sentenced to jail as a result of his refusal to obey an injuction. Upon appeal, *In Re Debs*, 158 U.S. 564 (1895), the Supreme Court said the government had the power " . . . to remove all obstructions upon highways, natural or artificial, to the passage of interstate commerce or the carrying of the mail. . . ." (Mueller, 1949, p. 177).

[7] Section 6. "That the labor of a human being is not a commodity or article of commerce . . . nor shall . . . [labor organizations] . . .or members therefore, be held or construed to be illegal combinations or conspiracies in restraint of trade, under the antitrust laws."

prises of American economic history, and these, along with labor's grievances, were the stuff of popular political rhetoric.

Thus legislation in favor of those who worked with their hands for their livelihoods in this country was not a bounty bestowed from above by a privileged class that ruled *den Staat*. The courts might drag their feet, but the movement became, finally, irresistible. Other states followed Indiana's example, and in 1898 Federal legislation, the Erdman Act, forbade yellow-dog contracts in railroad labor disputes. The Erdman Act was effectively nullified by the courts in *Adair* v. *United States* (1908), but the commerce clause made its appearance there for a moment. It would return in great boots in 1935.

With World War I, the balance shifted considerably. The Wilson Democrats used the powers of a wartime government to promote labor's cause. Already in 1916, the Adamson Act had established the 8-hour day in the railroads. In the same year, the Child Labor Act was passed by Congress. In wartime America, U.S. attorneys were ordered to defend union organizers. The government encouraged union organization in Federal employments, and a War Labor Board was established to arbitrate disputes. The courts fought back against these pressures. In 1905, in *Lochner* v. *New York*,, the Supreme Court had held that state laws limiting hours were interference with contract. Now *Hammer* v. *Dagenhart* (1918) overturned the Child Labor Act, *Hitchman Coal and Coke* v. *Mitchell* (1917) upheld the yellow-dog contract once more, and in 1923 the Court overturned the District of Columbia's effort to fix minimum wages for women and children in *Adkins* v. *Children's Hospital*. Not all of labor's gains were lost. In particular, government operation of the railroads ultimately produced a separate peace with railroad workers after the war in the Railway Labor Act of 1926. Its Railway Labor Board was a survivor of earlier arbitration boards, the War Labor Board, and was the precursor of the National Labor Board and the National Labor Relations Board (Hughes, 1977; Millis and Montgomery, 1945).

Momentum was regained with the onset of the Great Depression. First came Norris LaGuardia in 1931, later followed by the famous Section 7(a) of the NIRA which made collective bargaining mandatory with "representatives of their own choosing" between workers and employers adhering to the NRA industry codes. One has little trouble comprehending the role of Section 7(a). If the Federal government, in the interests of price and production stability, was to be the sponsor of ubiquitous and enforced cartelization of industry, given our background history, some system of mandatory collective bargaining was necessary for industrial peace, if for no other reason. There were, of course, the standard arguments that wage maintenance would support incomes and consumption. When the NIRA was overturned, Section 7(a) was thought to be protected by the commerce clause, and, accordingly, Section 1 of the NLRA invoked the commerce clause (again and again) as its warrant. That worked; in the test case,

Chief Justice Hughes relied on the commerce clause to uphold the act (Stern, 1946).

But mandatory collective bargaining was only half of the New Deal labor package. Following *West Coast Hotel* v. *Parrish* (1937), which upheld the minimum-wage law of Washington State, a federal law was now written setting maximum hours and minimum wages under the commerce clause, and as expressed in the Fair Labor Standards Act (1938). This legislation was the end of a long line of legal exegesis and litigation. In an enormous sweep of historical development, we had come full circle, in a way, back to Queen Elizabeth's *Statute of Artificers and Apprentices* (1562), which had also set labor standards. In that law, minimum hours were specified, with wages set by local authorities, and employment itself was made mandatory. It seems to have been our destiny to have these matters regulated. Nineteenth-century economic development saw the nadir of positive public regulation, but dissatisfaction with the results of the competitive labor market finally yielded to federal regulation in the Great Depression.

These solutions to problems of labor organization, wages, and hours have produced, in their turn, entirely new problems that we now confront and try to meet with further regulation. When set against the full history, I confess I cannot conceive of an outcome which excludes regulation—not with our history and commonlaw proceedings. Whether for or against labor, whether active or dormant, government regulation has always been there. Regulation of prices and wages was of ancient commonlaw origin, but our governments insisted upon the escalation of controls to the federal level. As Robert Stern (1946) wrote: "There would appear to be no difference in the constitutional power to protect interstate commerce against unduly high prices, as in the Sherman Act, and in excessively low prices, as in the New Deal legislation." The tradition was well known and had been enforced by the Supreme Court in *Munn* v. *Illinois*. The commerce power, although sometimes restrained, had been used successfully by 1933 to sustain new departures (Stern, 1946). The power was there, and it was used. A great fruition came during the New Deal to establish collective labor power, but I think some similar outcome would have come in any case. Labor unions with protected rights and powers exist in all noncommunist industrial countries. Our system contains peculiarities that are in accord with our traditions. Whether the system produced by the New Deal is the best one conceivable is another matter.

AGENCY NONMARKET CONTROLS

Proliferation of agency control was a hallmark of the New Deal era, and, together with the Executive Office's transmogrification by Executive Order 8248, in 1939 (Hess, 1976; Liebhafsky, 1971; Sherwood, 1950), the two sources of bureaucratic growth have resulted in the vast edifice of direct detailed regulation we see in Washington today. The two nonmarket-control sectors permeate the entire economy. The Bureau of the Budget was transferred to the Executive Office from the Treasury, and in the course of time the Executive Office has become the center of Administration activism, especially in the economic and social spheres. New schemes, like the Office of Economic Opportunity, can be tried out there, perhaps to be shifted later to permanent agencies and departments. It can be argued that the modern Executive Office is truly a New Deal innovation: It has grown into a regulatory power (of varying success) separate from the independent agencies and the other branches of government. It is designed to serve the desires of the Chief Executive and his closest associates with more freedom and discretion than can be achieved by the independent regulatory agencies. In the Executive Office, the officials are all the President's men. The style of the Roosevelt presidency has been continued by his successors. This had not been so following the reigns of Jackson, Lincoln, and Wilson—our earlier Napoleonic figures in the White House. So the councils and offices of the EOP have become a necessary bureaucratic palace guard. Had Nixon succeeded in covering the entire edifice with the mantle of executive privilege, we might now be facing a far more powerful regulatory device in the Executive Office than we have ever known.

It should be stressed that the extension of agency control during the 1930s was different from the innovation of controls. By 1933, the "founding fathers" of agency control, the ICC, FTC, FRS, FPC, and others, were already of age. The independent regulatory agency had been an accepted paradigm for nonmarket control long before the New Deal, but suddenly it could be elaborated endlessly. As in the case of the establishment of new labor standards, and union power by the federal government we may ask, What were the options? If we are not going to allow the "decision of the market" to allocate resources, what decision-making unit will we choose?

In our case, ancient tradition provided a ready-made answer (Hughes, 1976). The special control body was the common-law tradition, and it would not be successfully challenged. A profusion of such controls existed in the states[8] and since 1887, had been in Washington in small numbers. The law would uphold that which had always been. On the face of it, agency control is an unlikely candidate. For what is to be determined the public interest—after the public's own expression of its interest via the market mechanism has been rejected (Green, 1973; Hughes, 1977; Kahn, 1970; Liebhafsky, 1971; Scherer, 1970). The special regulatory agency goes back to the Middle Ages in Anglo-American legal history. Whether it was a special commission, a regular body like the parish vestrymen (in England), township selectmen in the colonial era (buttressed by a small army of

---

[8] Twenty-five states had railroad regulatory commissions before the ICC was established in 1887 (Robert E. Cushman 1937).

wardens, watchers, gaugers, and reeves), or county and state commissions, the general philosophy ruled that a small body of specially charged persons of wisdom can detect the public interest and secure it by coercion. In its earliest existence, the idea had some legitimacy. Even if public interests were not spelled out in law, the communications problem might be solved in small communities with limited kinds of economic activities and where the relevant "public" was limited to property-owners, rate-payers, freemen, citizens in good standing or the like. In colonial New England, for example, a town meeting (with a vote taken after a debate) or just an informal polling by the relevant authorities might produce a viable consensus.

The problem of communication becomes overwhelming, though, in a modern economy unless the public interest is narrowly defined in legislation, which it almost never is. The common-law rule for prices of services and goods in public callings was "reasonable," and that word is still used in disputes over public services. The courts tried to determine reasonable freight rates, then the ICC was charged with discovering them. Once the desires of those being regulated are also admitted into the formulation, compromise is the obvious way out, and muddle is the most likely result. There is also the problem that, even with the most modern polling devices, the public may not even know, until it is too late, what its interest is on many issues. One recalls that 82% originally supported the American effort in Vietnam, and Lyndon Johnson was buoyed up by that expression of the public interest.

Successful or not, the agencies of nonmarket control are long-lived and grow similar to a coral reef. Each agency represents some kind of historical solution (or nonsolution) of a specific problem. Over time, Washington has become a museum of these artifacts which are, in aggregate, a form of permanent government. However, it is a government which was planned by no one at any point in time, representing no general interest, uncoordinated, and quite possibly, not fully understood by any single person or body of persons, even though each agency could conceivably understand its own charge. But can an agency like the ICC, with more than an estimated 40-odd trillion freight rates to administer, really know what it is doing?[9] By the 1930s the enveloping power of agency regulation was well understood but not the alternatives (if any) to the creation of new agencies. An executive document of 1937 begins (Cushman, 1937):

> There is high respect . . . for the independent commission as a device for Federal regulation. There exists a strong inclination to use this method for handling new regulatory jobs as they emerge. At the same time, the multiplication of these independent bodies tends inevitably toward a decentralized and chaotic administrative system. They are areas of unaccountability. They occupy important fields of administration

---

[9] In 1973 new tariff applications reached the ICC at an annual rate of 270,000 per year.

fastest growing kind of nonmarket control in the 1970s. But, mainly, the New Deal control agencies created were of the traditional kind, one per industry: SEC for securities, CAB for airlines, REA for rural power. The big aggregate control, centered on the Council of Economic Advisers under the Employment Act of 1946, was not really New Deal in time or intellectual technology. The triumph of an activist fiscal policy, in theory, together with the fiscal muscle to maintain the steady growth of a managerial and entrepreneurial federal government, was realized by the World War II pay-as-you-earn income tax. The New Deal experience was used as the base for the modern system of controlled capitalism.

SOCIAL INSURANCE

A year ago a Soviet economist asked me why our government tolerates so much unemployment? I explained to him that it was not always so. Our tradition in these matters came from the English, and they did not view unemployment kindly. Among the basic laws at our founding were the two Elizabethan statutes, the *Statute of Artificers and Apprentices*, which I have already mentioned, and the *Act for Punishment of Rogues, Vagabonds, and Sturdy Beggars* (39 Eliz. I, c. 4.) of 1597. And still evident was Henry VIII's law of 1535 concerning charitable alms (27 Henry VIII, c. 25) which provided whipping for the first offense of vagabondage, the "gristle of his right ear cut off" for the second offense, and execution as a felon for the third. All persons not among the privileged orders were to labor. Children were to be apprenticed. Massachusetts laws of 1646, 1655, and 1657 empowered magistrates to imprison all "idle persons" with ten lashes upon entering the jails and to compel them to labor in order to earn " . . . necessary bread and water, or other mean food" (Whitmore, 1889). William Penn wanted all children in Pennsylvania at age 12 to be taught trades " . . . to the end none may be idle, but the poor may work to live and the rich, if they become poor, may not want" (Hughes, 1973). Philadelphia's almshouse, the receptacle for those without work, was called the House of Employment. Even the job of overseer of the poor in that place in the City of Brotherly Love was compulsory (Allison and Penrose, 1887). In Maryland, every county had an almshouse or workhouse, and the trustees were ordered to compel the poor to labor (Mereness, 1901). Jefferson, boasting of Virginia's lack of beggars noted that "Vagabonds, without visible property or vocation, are placed in workhouses, where they are well clothed, fed, lodged, and made to labor" (Jefferson, 1788). I think my Soviet friend would have found these stout American origins congenial.

Even in living memory, vagabond laws were enforced against the unemployed to compel them to accept work at going wages. Administrative methods still are used to enforce labor upon those on "welfare," e.g., AFDC mothers (Pivon and Cloward, 1971), and President Carter (*New York Times*, 1977) recently called for a work requirement for those receiving assistance. However, it is no doubt true that we must appear weakened when compared to our sturdy ancestors. As the economy became both more affluent overall and cyclical unemployment left millions out of work periodically, there were both the means and the sound political reasons to find methods to deal with unemployment that were less draconian and more consistent with the elementary civil rights of voters. We joined other modern nations in 1935 when we made unemployment insurance compulsory in selected employments in the Social Security Act.

In that same legislation, we created the beginnings of comprehensive federal pensions for the aged together with federal obligations to assist in care for the aged, infirm, and indigent. This assumption of federal power was a radical change in our practice, for we abandoned the age-old principle that such matters were best left to local authority exclusively. No one would argue that the federal intervention here was a solution to *any* of these problems or that the problems were new in the 1930s. The tradition of local responsibility for poor relief goes back to the statute of 1535 of Henry VIII. The tradition was honored in colonial America and in the Federal period (Hughes, 1976). Ricardo (1963) celebrated the wisdom of it in his *Principles*, adding the elegant warning:

> Each parish raises a separate fund for the support of its own poor . . . It is to this cause that we must ascribe the fact of the poor laws not having yet absorbed all of the net revenue of the country, . . . If by law every human being wanting support could be sure to obtain it, and obtain it in such a degree as to make life tolerably comfortable, theory would lead us to expect that all other taxes together would be light compared with the single one of the poor rates. The principle of gravitation is not more certain than the tendency of such laws to change wealth into misery and weakness; to call away the exertions of labour from every object, except that of providing mere subsistence; to confound all intellectual distinction, to busy the mind continually in supplying the body's wants; until at last all classes should be infected with the plague of universal poverty [Ricardo, D. *Principles of political economy and taxation*. Homewood, Ill.: Richard Irwin, 1963, p. 54].

During the 19th century and until the 1930s, the principle of local responsibility was maintained, was fought for by Hoover, and survives today in the federal government's reliance upon grants-in-aid to the states in these matters. But the federal government did finally intervene on an emergency basis from 1933 on and then, in the Social Security Act, staked out a territory of its own. With the addition of medicare and the explosion of AFDC and other social security expenditures since 1964, the federal obligation has enlarged enormously.[13] The public assistance "firms" in HEW are thriving.

One must credit the New Deal with these innovations. Moreover, as techniques of social regulation, they are potentially threatening to elementary civil rights in

---

[13] Piven and Cloward (1971) Appendix, Table 1, HEW figures show a 58% national increase in AFDC cases in 1964–1969 alone.

ways that dwarf any such threats in the past. I am not saying it is wrong to aid the poor or to provide social security pensions. But, if we are tracing the roots of regulation in the New Deal, surely these are most potent. These measures were adopted in the presence of great social stress, partly for the purest humanitarian reasons, and partly because they seemed the acme of scientific social thought. The idea of "social insurance" is celebrated in all the elementary economics textbooks. Yet these measures require certain social status and certain behavior among recipients. The social security number itself is the American pigtail, enabling our modern Manchus to capture conveniently all relevant data on every person. Stored data can be used for social and political ends, as well as merely for a bank of IRS information.

One must ask again if these steps were inevitable? What would have happened in Hoover's second term? The idea of unemployment insurance was widespread in the country before the 1930s, and some voluntary plans were actually in existence (79 in 1931 covering 226,000 persons). Enlightened opinion favored such insurance after Lord Beveridge's book, *Unemployment, A Problem of Industry*, was published in 1908. In the 1920s bills attempting to establish compulsory systems had been introduced in state legislatures (Gagliardo, 1949). The Swope Plan (Frederick, 1931), which attracted wide attention in the early 1930s, explicitly involved federal participation in both its unemployment insurance and retirement pension sections. Gerard Swope was president of General Electric, and his scheme was touted by industrialists and politicians alike as an "American System." The traditional system of poor relief for the aged, infirm, and destitute had been the creation of men living in a tiny agrarian society, and it is difficult to imagine that almshouses, workhouses, prisons, state home-relief, and mothers-aid pensions could cope with problems on the scale we now experience. The evidence is that these systems had broken down hopelessly in the 1930s (Schlesinger, 1957; Shannon, 1960). Other industrial countries had adopted techniques of their own to cope with these problems, and I think our time had more or less come in the 1930s, no matter who was in the White House.

The New Deal can be faulted in the piece-meal, unequal way these problems were handled. The continued adherence to the tradition of local control produced fantastic problems [e.g., massive rural-urban migrations (Pivon and Cloward, 1971)], for posterity. The avoidance of legitimate insurance principles left Social Security wide-open in later years for all sorts of changes, innovation, and irregularities that could not be financed by the original scheme. The Social Security tax itself has become a way of raising income taxes "benevolently" that lets our political leaders off the hook for the financial consequences of their policies.

One could go on in detail in this vein, but I will leave that to others as my charge is historical. I must add, in defense of the New Deal leaders, that they were aware of the deficiencies in much that was done in 1935, but they wanted the bill, and paid the price to get it. The result is a program that satisfied few indeed but that, at least, is consistent with the rest of our regulatory nonsystem. When Tugwell protested to Roosevelt of the regressivity of payroll taxes, the president defended them as good politics: "... those taxes were never a problem of economics. They are politics all the way through" (Schlesinger, 1959).

CONCLUSIONS

The New Deal did not end the depression of the 1930s. Moreover, the real fiscal revolution came from the pay-as-you-earn personal income tax of World War II. That, not the New Deal innovations, made ideas like those behind the Employment Act of 1946 practicable. However, if a "modern" government is defined as one which is more deeply involved in regulating individual lives in the interest of higher objectives than in the mere protection of personal freedom, then one must admit that the New Deal made a significant contribution. Even so, there is more in the New Deal of continuity than of originality. Even the process of expanding the federal power at the expense of persons and other levels of government was long abuilding before 1933, although there is no doubt of the acceleration of the process by the New Deal. Apart from the centralization of control functions in the federal government, I believe the New Deal's main contribution to American history was the introduction of government economic activism for its own sake in peacetime as a successful political program. The style has remained with us and is demanded of all federal administrations.

Is there any evidence that the New Deal statesmen would have dismantled the dysfunctional parts of their creation had it not been for World War II? I believe the answer to the last question must be No. The Employment Act, of 1946, was really radical at the federal level, and many other federal nonmarket controls have been, and still are being, created. The record shows that, before, during, and since the 1930s, we have preferred an economy "controlled" by the political power, no matter how poorly it performs, to a free economy. We seem to see economic freedom as risky, and we seem to be very risk averse. Rexford Tugwell, no friend of *laissez faire* in the 1930s, knew this, but he also knew the powerful American tradition of nonmarket controls and feared that the tradition would win out over any efforts at planning and quantitative control. He did not fear the power of free enterprise. He did not believe there would be a powerful resurgence of free-market capitalism. He feared the power of the tradition (Luechtenburg, 1963; Schlesinger, 1960; Tugwell, 1968). He was right, and the tradition ruled. Until now, there has been no serious move to impose "planning" by the federal government. The "market economy" remains subject to the restraints and regulations imposed by that curious combination of conservatives and liberals who see *both* antitrust and agency control as desirable governors of economic activity. I am unaware of any serious proposals to reduce the amount of federal involvement in personal affairs characteristic of the Federal Security Administration and the expanding concerns of the HEW entrepreneurs. So like the poor, the New Deal is always with us.

ACKNOWLEDGMENT

I am indebted to my colleagues, F. M. Scherer, Joel Mokyr, and Louis Cain, for criticisms.

REFERENCES

Allison, E. P., and Penrose, B. *Philadelphia 1681-1887.* Baltimore: Johns Hopkins Univ. Press, 1887. Pp. 37-40, 68, 108.
Berkowitz, E. and McQuaid, K. Businessman and bureaucrat: The evolution of the American social welfare system, 1900-1940. *Journal of Economic History,* 1978, March.
Cushman, R. E. *The problem of the independent regulatory commissions.* Studies on Administrative Management in the Government of the United States, the President's Committee on Administrative Management. Washington, D.C.: U.S. Government Printing Office, 1937. P. 3.
Fausold, M. L. President Hoover's farm policies 1929-1933. *Agricultural History,* 1977, *51,* 368-372.
Frederick, J. G., ed. *The Swope plan: details, criticisms, analysis.* New York: The Business Course, 1931.
Gagliardo, D. *American social insurance.* New York: Harper, 1949.
Goodrich, C. *Government promotion of American canals and railroads 1800-1890.* New York: Columbia Univ. Press, 1960.
Goodrich, C., ed. *The government and the economy, 1783-1861,* part 3. Indianapolis: Bobbs-Merrill, 1967.
Gray, H. M. *The Journal of Land and Public Utility Economics,* Feb. 1940. (Reprinted in the *American Economic Association Readings in the Public Control of Industry.* Philadelphia: Blakiston, 1942.)
Green, M. J., ed. *The monopoly makers,* New York: Grossman, 1973.
Haitus, F., Mak, J., and Walton, G. M. *Western river transportation.* Baltimore: Johns Hopkins Press, 1975.
Hawley, E. W. *The New Deal and the problem of monopoly.* Englewood Cliffs: Princeton Univ. Press, 1966.
Hess, S. *Organizing the presidency.* Washington, D.C.: Brookings Institution, 1976.
Hicks, J. D. *The populist revolt.* University of Nebraska Press, 1961.
Hill, F. G. *Roads, rails and waterways: The Army engineers and early transportation.* Norman: University of Oklahoma Press, 1957.
Historical Statistics of the United States. Washington, D.C.: USGPO, 1960.
Horwitz, M. *The transformation of American law 1780-1860.* Cambridge: Harvard University Press, 1977. Pp. 186-187.
Hughes, J. *The vital few: American economic progress and its protagonists.* New York: Oxford Univ. Press, 1973. P. 139.
Hughes, J. R. T. *Social control in the colonial economy.* Charlottesville: The Univ. Press of Virginia, 1976. Pp. 96-111.

Hughes, J. *The governmental habit: Economic controls from colonial times to the present.* New York: Basic Books, 1977.

Jefferson, T. *Notes on the state of Virginia.* London: John Stockdale, 1788.

Jensen, M. C. and Meckling, W. H. Can the corporation be saved? *Master in Business Administration*, March, 1977.

Joint Economic Committee, *Subsidies and subsidylike programs.* Washington, D.C.: United States Government Printing Office, 1960, 86th Congress, 2nd Session, pp. 28-29.

Joint Economic Committee, *Subsidy and subsidy-effect programs of the U.S. government,* Washington, D.C.: United States Government Printing Office, 1965, 89th Congress, 1st Session. Pp. 11-19.

Jouvenal, B. De. *On power: Its history and the nature of its growth.* Boston: Beacon Press, 1962. P. 157.

Kahn, A. E. *The Economics of Regulation.* New York: Wiley, 1970.

Kent, J. *Commentaries on American law,* vol. 2. Boston: Little Brown, 1884.

Krooss, H. *Executive opinion: What business leaders said and thought, 1920s-1960s.* New York: Doubleday, 1970.

Leuchtenburg, W. E. *Franklin D. Roosevelt and the New Deal.* New York: Harper, 1963. Pp. 162-164.

Liebhafsky, H. H. *American Government and Business.* New York: Wiley, 1971. Pp. 410-412.

Locklin, P. *Economics of transportation.* Homewood, Ill.: Richard Irwin, 1947. Pp. 741-749.

Loewe v. *Lawlor*, 208 U.S. 274 (1908).

Mereness, N. B. *Maryland as a proprietary province.* New York: Macmillan, 1901. Pp. 136, 403-406.

Millis, H. A. and Montgomery, R. E. *Organized Labor* New York: McGraw Hill, 1945. P. 509.

Mueller, S. J. *Labor law and legislation.* New York: South-Western Pub. Co., 1949. Pp. 20-35.

National Resources Planning Board, *The Economic effects of the federal public works expenditures, 1933-1938.* Washington, D. C.: United States Government Printing Office, 1940.

New York Times, August 7, 1977.

Oklahoma v. *Atkinson & Co.*, 313 U.S. 508 (1941) 525.

Pearce, C. A. *Trade Associations Survey.* TNEC Monograph No. 18. Washington, D.C.: United States Government Printing Office, 1941.

Perlman, S. *A Theory of the labor movement.* New York: Augustus Kelley, 1949. P. 196, n.1.

Piven, F. F. and Cloward, R. A. *Regulating the poor: The Functions of public welfare.* New York: Vintage Books, 1971. Chapters 4-6.

Ricardo, D. *Principles of political economy and taxation.* Homewood, Ill.: Richard Irwin, 1963. P. 54.

Scherer, F. M. *Industrial market structure and economic performance.* Chicago: Rand McNally, 1970. Chapter 22.

Schlesinger, A. M., Jr. *The age of Roosevelt: The coming of the New Deal.* Boston: Houghton Mifflin, 1959.

Schlesinger, A. M., Jr., *The age of Roosevelt: The crisis of the old order.* Boston: Houghton Mifflin, 1957. Chapters IV-VII.

Schlesinger, A. M., Jr., *The age of Roosevelt: The politics of upheaval.* Boston: Houghton Mifflin, 1960.

Schultz, G. R., and Dam, K. W. *Economic policy beyond the headlines.* New York: Norton, 1977.

Shannon, D. A. *The Great Depression.* Englewood Cliffs: Prentice Hall, 1960.

Sherwood, R. E. *Roosevelt and Hopkins.* Vol. I. New York: Bantam Books, 1950. Vol. 1. Pp. 63-69.

Simpson, S. P. The interstate commerce commission and railroad consolidating. *Harvard Law Review, XLIII,* 1929-1930.

Smithies, A. The American economy in the thirties. *American Economic Review,* 1946, *XXVI,* May.

Stein, H. *The fiscal revolution in America.* Chicago: Univ. of Chicago Press, 1969.

Stern, R. L. The commerce clause and the national economy 1933-1946. *Harvard Law Review,* 1946, *LIX,* May.

Thorpe, F. N., ed. *The federal and state constitutions, colonial charters, and other organic laws of the states, territories, and colonies now or heretofore forming the United States of America,* Washington, D.C., United States Government Printing Office, 1909. Virginia charter of 1606, p. 3787; charter of 1609, pp. 3799-3800.

Tugwell, R. G. *The brains trust.* New York: Viking, 1968. Pp. 128-129, 144-145, 124-175, 405-407.

United States Customs Laws 1789-1895, Washington, D.C., United States Government Printing Office, 1896, p. 9.

Weidenbaum, M. L. *Business, government, and the public.* Englewood Cliffs: Prentice Hall, 1977.

Whitmore, W., ed. *The colonial laws of Massachusetts.* Boston: Rockwell and Churchill, 1889. Pp. 138-139.

Wilcox, C. *Public policies toward business.* Homewood, Ill.: Richard Irwin, 1960. P. 429.

Discussion

PETER TEMIN

"I will argue in this chapter," Hughes says, "that it was not what was done in the 1930s, but *where* it was done that mattered. It was not primarily the imposition of more nonmarket controls over persons, but the federal assumption of the power to impose them together with its prolific activism in the economy, that made the New Deal such a critical change in American history, that qualified it for the word *revolutionary* (p. 32, this volume). Hughes then goes on to give four separate examples of the process he is describing. He chronicles the growth of federal subsidies and expenditures (one category), federal regulatory agencies, federal support for unions, and what Hughes calls social insurance.

My problem with the chapter is not with what it says, but with what it omits. As Hughes says: "*How* it was done is not so important as *why* (p. 32, this volume). But Hughes concentrates almost exclusively on how, leaving the question of why implicit in his various narratives. I will make three brief passes in this comment at the question of why the New Deal took the shape it did, presenting three observations at differing levels of abstraction.

The first observation rests on a legal distinction. Hughes refers to many legal arguments that were used to justify and defend New Deal measures. Two arguments seem particularly important: the Commerce Clause, that figured so prominently in labor legislation—the NIRA and the NLRA— and its court tests, and police power, that was the basis of much of the regulatory legislation in the Depression.

The use of these two arguments reveals two different conceptions of the expansion of federal government activity. The police-power argument speaks to the relationship of government and the individual. It addresses the question of individual freedom, not the question of the level of government that should dominate. The Commerce Clause, in contrast, is concerned directly with the allocations of functions within the government. With police power, the question is whether to regulate. With the Commerce Clause, the question is who should regulate.

There is no one-to-one linkage between legal arguments and ideology. A detailed study of the legal basis of the New Deal would not inevitably reveal the logic of the regulatory process. Nevertheless, such a study could go far toward disentangling some of the loose strands. Hughes describes the use of federal subsidies to appropriate power both from individuals and from lower levels of government (see p. 38, this volume). Examination of state and local government activity is needed to reveal which was more typical. However, careful attention to the underlying legal arguments might reveal what policy makers thought they were doing.

The second observation grows out of the obvious matter of timing. The New Deal was a response to the Depression. Yet the Depression itself hardly figures in Hughes' discussion. There is no suggestion that he has forgotten about it or that he is denying its existence; scattered comments in the paper assure us to the contrary. Instead, the Depression simply does not figure importantly in Hughes' argument.

This is very strange. The New Deal was first and foremost an attempt to end the Depression. Its lack of success in this dimension cannot be allowed to blind us to the aims with which it was promulgated. The difference between economic theory then and now must not blur our perception of motivation in the 1930s.

For example, our familiar distinction between *microeconomics* and *macroeconomics* postdates the Depression. In fact, it is the result of theoretical attempts to explain the Depression. At the time of the New Deal, economic theory stood as a unit. People reasoned from similar premises when thinking about the economy as a whole and when thinking about individual industries, and they did not distinguish two sets of policy tools according to the scope of their economic goals.

From our point of view, the New Deal represented an attempt to solve macroeconomic problems with microeconomic tools. As such, it was doomed to failure. However, if one looks only at the microeconomic aspects of the New Deal— using our modern distinction—one will miss many of the reasons why the New Deal was enacted.

The National Industrial Recovery Act, which was passed in June, 1933, as part of the first New Deal, is a case in point. It represented an attempt to end or alleviate the Depression by restraining "excessive" competition and raising wages. In modern terms, it represented a microeconomic policy to deal with a macroeconomic problem. It was similar, therefore, to recent measures to combat "stagflation" that try to generate employment without raising wages or to reduce wage inflation without creating more unemployment.

A generation of historians agreed that the NIRA was ineffective in curing the Depression. After all, the Depression did not end when the New Deal was passed. The historians concentrated on the microeconomic effects of the industry codes, talking about the hours' provisions, the limitation of competition, changes in wage differentials, and other microeconomic aspects of the NIRA. They could ignore its macroeconomic impact because it was thought to be minor or nonexistent.

Hughes follows in this tradition, and the NIRA appears in his paper because of its microeconomic impact. However, a discussion of the NIRA that omits reference to the macroeconomic aims of its supporters misses the larger part of the process by which it took shape. A fortiori, a discussion of the Wagner Act that does not trace its origins through the NIRA and the macroeconomic concerns of the first New Deal comes perilously close to being Hamlet without the prince.

The third observation about the sources of the New Deal grows out of the change in economic theory just alluded to. The Depression was unprecedented and unanticipated. Economic theory of the time argued that the private market would allocate resources to the best interests of all. A growing literature in the 1920s had pinpointed exceptions to this general rule, but none of them was important enough to invalidate the system as a whole. The Depression, by contrast, threw the whole theory into doubt.

Faith in the market was replaced in part by faith in professional guidance. Despite the bewildering diversity of federal action in the New Deal, the expert regulatory agency can be regarded as the archetypal creation. The few agencies existing at the onset of the Depression were joined by many younger cousins, who have been joined again by a new generation in our day. The agencies implemented the recommendations of professional experts in their appointed areas.

The professions grew in the late nineteeenth century. Their growth can be seen in part as a response to the rise of large-scale business firms in which the middle class tried to preserve and gain status. Professional associations formed a counterweight to large corporations, enlisting government aid in the form of licensing and other exclusive privileges whenever possible (Friedman, 1965; Hofstadter, 1955).

The distinction between professional and other occupations was then and has remained primarily educational. Middle-class, professional work required postsecondary education then; it requires postgraduate education now. As a result of this attention to education, and as a result of the advances in knowledge generated by the growing educational establishment, the professions increasingly were seen as carriers of advanced knowledge and skill. The skills were necessary for the work of the professionals. The knowledge became identified with the vanguard of civilization, giving the professionals a special place in society. They became authoritative problem solvers for society (Freidson, 1970, 1978; Gilb, 1966; Lieberman, 1970).

This long-term trend of increasing reliance on professionals to solve problems was accentuated by the Depression. Ordinary people, interacting through the market, were no longer seen as competent determinants of society's best interests. The market no longer appeared able to translate myriad individual, ordinary desires into the social optimum. Professionals were needed to discover the knowledge that the market did not reveal, and they were needed to design policies to force the market away from its suboptimal equilibrium to a more beneficial position.

Implicit in this argument was the assumption that professionals would act "in the public interest." Their professional commitment, it was thought, would outweigh their desires for personal gain, leading them to consider the interests of society as a whole. Given this assumption and the advanced knowledge and skills of the professionals, it was natural to delegate decision making to them.

Rules for marketing financial securities were determined by experts resident in a regulatory agency. Rules for marketing medicinal drugs were determined similarly. Power transmission and communications were regulated by specialized agencies. Without wishing to ignore or denigrate the other forms of federal actions of the New Deal, these are the archetypal actions. As Hughes states, the expansion of government subsidies and expenditures was as much a shift of decision making into the federal government as was the formation of regulatory agencies.

Let me cite a specific example here, too. A bill to revise the Pure Food and Drug Act of 1906 was submitted to Congress in the early days of the New Deal. It remained in Congress for 5 years before it was passed in 1938. The new law strengthened the FDA's control over drug labeling, but it did not restrict the availability of drugs to individuals. Any nonnarcotic drug at the time could be purchased without a prescription; an individual could choose whether he wanted to visit a doctor and get a prescription or go directly to a pharmacist and buy drugs without a doctor's aid. The administrative regulations issued in 1938 to enforce the law changed this. It created the class of prescription drugs which has become familiar to us today. After that date, some drugs—an increasing number after World War II—could be purchased only with a doctor's prescription. The assumption was that the professional doctor would make an informed choice in the individual's interest. This assumption was made by an expert federal agency. Public acquiescence in this assumption and in the way it was introduced into public policy reveals the extent to which expert, professional authority had been accepted (Temin, 1979).

The use of professionals to make decisions for society has come under increasing attack in our day. Economists attack professionals as monopolists who have increased their incomes at the expense of the rest of us by restricting entry into their chosen domain. Political scientists attack professionals as private governments that make decisions on our behalf without our representation. Radicals criticize professionals for their emphasis on credentials, for their restriction of our freedom and for the costs of their actions on society. Conservatives also criticize professionals, for the waste involved in their decisions and for their inability to restructure their professions and agencies to keep pace with the changing needs of society.

But this criticism has come to the fore amidst the generation after the Depression. For the Depression generation itself, the lure of professional decisions was irresistible, and the pursuit of this goal led to the expansion of federal government activity that Hughes chronicles.

It would caricature history to say that people ceased to believe in the market all at once. Belief in the normative properties of the free market had been eroding since the late nineteenth century (Fine, 1956). And many people still believe in the efficacy of the market today. (Significantly, those economists who think this way also deny or blur the distinction between micro- and macroeconomics.) Nevertheless, the Depression witnessed an important acceleration of the trend away from market solutions.

Similarly, the New Deal cannot be seen simply as a set of economically expansionist ideas. Many New Dealers, of whom Tugwell may be the most famous or infamous, saw the Depression as an opportunity to implement long-desired changes in the structure of the economy. As the legal arguments of the 1930s suggest and Hughes' presentation shows, many changes involved a reallocation of government responsibility as much as an expansion.

These three observations, therefore, each capture only a partial aspect of the New Deal, and some catch even that partial view only imperfectly. Nevertheless, generalizations like these need to be added to the specifics in Hughes' discussion to draw out their implications.

REFERENCES

Fine, S. *Laissez-faire and general welfare state.* Ann Arbor: University of Michigan Press, 1956.

Freidson, E. *Profession of medicine: A study of the sociology of applied knowledge.* New York: Dodd, Mead and Co., 1970.

Freidson, E. "Are professions necessary?" MIT Seminar, April 14, 1978.

Friedman, L. "Freedom of contract and occupational licensing 1890-1910: A legal and social study," *California Law Review*, 1965, *53*, 487-534.

Gilb, C. *Hidden hierarchies: The professions and government.* New York: Harper and Row, 1966.

Hofstadter, R. *The age of reform.* New York: Random House, 1955.

Lieberman, J. *Tyranny of the experts.* New York: Walker, 1970.

Temin, P. The origin of compulsory drug prescriptions. *Journal of Law and Economics,* 1979, *22,* 91-105.

Chapter 4

The Robinson-Patman Act: A New Deal for Small Business

KENNETH G. ELZINGA

On June 19, 1936, the world's attention was focused on a number of events. The Prime Minister of England said to the House of Commons, "Chancellor Hitler has told us that he wishes peace, and if a man tells me that, as I have said before, I wish to try it out." In the United States, Max Schmeling stunned millions of Joe Louis fans with his knockout victory over the Brown Bomber in Yankee Stadium. The academic world was occupied by a commencement address by Walter Lippmann in which he proposed a total ban on professors in government. Lippman said, "If the professors try to run the government, we shall end up by having the government run the professors." The Republicans had just given their presidential nomination to Governor Alf Landon; in a remarkable display of optimism, he accepted. And three million veterans had begun spending their "Bonus Bills," following what was called "the greatest pay day in the history of the nation."

It's little wonder that when, on that day, Franklin Delano Roosevelt signed into law the Robinson–Patman Act,[1] the event went scarcely noticed in the press. However, since its birth in obscurity, the act has gained a durable prominence.[2]

This prominence has not been due to the act's allocative effects, for, in this regard, it is dwarfed by other New Deal programs. But within the context of New Deal philosophy and the current interest in regulatory reform, Robinson-Patman is particularly worthy of inspection, for three reasons. First, the act is an especially characteristic example of New Deal legislation, almost an archetype. Second, the recent history of the act's enforcement shows it to be a precursor of regulatory reform. Finally, a misunderstanding of the economic practice which provoked the act continues to be an obstacle to a full reform of this particular piece of New Deal legislation.

ROBINSON-PATMAN AS NEW DEAL LEGISLATION

The Robinson-Patman Act has all four characteristics associated with the New Deal legislative ethos. First, the statute represents a distrust of purely voluntary contractual arrangements and manifests a willingness on the part of the federal government to modify the central nervous system of a free enterprise economy: the setting of price. Under the act, primarily sellers, but also buyers, must consider the potential liability of granting or seeking selective price cuts. Government sanction is not the only threat to noncompliance. Violating the Robinson-Patman Act can entail private treble damage suits.

Since the act has gained such a strong presumption of illegality (upon a showing of price differences), it increases the cost of shading prices. A smaller quantity of price shading results. The law reduces price flexibility (Elzinga, 1976) and a seller's ability to enter new markets through price attractiveness (*National Dairy Products Corp.*, 1967).

A second New Deal characteristic of the Robinson-Patman Act is its design to elevate prices. The Robinson-Patman Act represented a microeconomic dovetailing with the macroeconomic view of the Roosevelt Brains Trust, namely that prices were too low and that any additional decrease in prices would further reduce incomes and exacerbate the malaise of the nation's economy. The propping up of prices was one of the tasks of the regulatory commissions that proliferated during the New Deal. Their concern was more often with price floors than ceilings, and the Robinson-Patman Act was in keeping with this spirit. Even more closely, the Robinson-Patman Act paralleled the subsequent federal legisla-

---

[1] Act of June 19, 1936, 49 Stat. 1526. The law prohibits certain forms of price discrimination on the part of sellers and prohibits buyers from being the recipient of certain price advantages.

[2] The act itself is lengthy and its interpretation and enforcement intricate. Two standard sources on the law and its development are Corwin D. Edwards (1959) and F. M. Rowe (1962). A recent explanation of the mechanics of the act is United States Department of Justice, *Report on the Robinson-Patman Act*, 1977, Chapter II.

tion allowing resale price maintenance agreements. The purpose of the so-called fair trade law, the Miller-Tydings Act of 1937,[3] was to maintain resale prices to customers.[4] The Robinson-Patman Act can be characterized as a fair trade law at the manufacturing level. Fair trade assisted, for example, the independent jewelry stores in competing against large retailers who could otherwise undersell them by virtue of their scale economies at the retailing level. The Robinson-Patman Act assisted the independent jewelers in a related way, by deterring the same large retailers from exploiting, through advantageous purchase terms, the economies that manufacturers sustained in selling to large buyers. Fair trade deterred price cuts at the retailing level; the Robinson-Patman Act deterred cuts at the manufacturing level.

Still another characteristic of the Robinson-Patman Act, not unlike other New Deal programs, was its hasty conception. The New Deal was a time of economic action *sans* careful weighing and consideration of the consequences. This is often taken to be one of the strengths of the era's policies. On March 4, 1978, the forty-fifth anniversary of the inauguration of Franklin Delano Roosevelt was celebrated in Washington, D.C. As part of a revealing and enchanting after dinner program, Senator Jennings Randolph of West Virginia, the only person still in Congress who overlapped with Roosevelt's assumption of the presidency, told of being invited to the White House, along with other new Congressmen, and of being instructed by the president on the importance of immediately pressing ahead with Roosevelt's legislative programs. One Congressman objected, "What if we make mistakes?" Roosevelt replied that mistakes would no doubt be made, but that action was required. Rexford Tugwell (1977) the economics professor Roosevelt plucked from Columbia University for his Brains Trust, wrote this about the times:

> We were too busy then to make accurate assessments. There was so much to do and so few hours in the days or days in the month that we hurried from one stint to another without much intermission. If we had not already thought about what had to be done, there was little possibility that we could catch up; but, of course, plans had been roughed out. The depression had provided the insistent motive. (p. xii)

Finally, the Robinson-Patman Act represents the element of New Deal philosophy that desired a return to the harmony of yesteryear. There is no evidence that Roosevelt desired a truly radical or regimented social order. He and his colleagues wanted to return the nation as much as possible to its predepression ways. The Robinson-Patman Act was an endeavor to preserve a distribution system that was being threatened. This system had had two structural characteris-

---

[3] 50 Stat. 693, 15 U.S.C.A. #1.
[4] By 1937, one year after Robinson-Patman, the Roosevelt administration was to become less receptive to (at least some) legislation which would raise relative prices. The Departments of Labor, Agriculture, Justice and the Treasury all protested Congressional proposals for fair trade legislation and, when the bill was eventually passed, Roosevelt considered its veto, waiting 9 days before reluctantly signing it. For an account of this episode see Ellis W. Hawley (1966).

tics. One was its three-tiered organization: goods flowed from manufacturer to independent wholesaler to independent retailer. The Robinson-Patman Act sought to protect the independent wholesaler from attempts by either manufacturers or retailers to integrate into the wholesaling function. At the retail end, the Robinson-Patman Act, along with fair trade, sought to preserve the independent retail outlet, the so-called "Mom and Pop" store. There was very little opposition in Congress to the merits of such a preservation. Congressman Jack Nichols of Oklahoma claimed:[5]

> You know there is a certain sentiment and romance about the corner or crossroads grocery store. There formerly, and there now, exists the skit and whittle club. You know, where the boys gather around the stove in the winter, sit around its red-hot fire, chew tobacco, spit on the bowl, and listen to it sizzle, and settle the problems of the Nation, and the problems of the community [pp. 106-107].

The Robinson-Patman Act was to maintain an atmosphere for skit and whittle.[6]

All that keeps the Robinson-Patman Act from being archetypal New Deal is its method of conception. The conventional image of the New Deal is that of a powerful president who, under the tutelage of his advice-giving Brains Trust, directs a willing if not subservient Congress to legislate a greatly expanded role for the federal government. This image is not wholly misleading, but it does not depict the birth of the Robinson-Patman Act. Its parents were Congress and the U.S. Wholesale Grocers' Association. Congressman Wright Patman, whose recent investigations of chain store buying practices had secured for him much press attention, was the logical namesake of the bill. Majority leader Joseph Robinson attached his imprimatur on the Senate side. The drafter of the bill was the legal counsel for the grocery wholesalers' association, H. B. Teegarden, who demurely encouraged the nation's retail trade associations to assume the public posture as parent. Thus, while the Robinson-Patman Act typifies the New Deal era and expands the involvement of the federal government in commerce, its impetus was not with Roosevelt and his advisors.[7]

---

[5] 80 Cong. Rec. 8135 as quoted in *Report on the Robinson-Patman Act* (United States Department of Justice, 1977). Someday, one conjectures, today's youngsters whose social life centers around the suburban shopping malls and strip centers of America will speak nostalgically of the necessity of these business institutions to the nation's social fabric.

[6] Exacerbating the sentiment in favor of small enterprise was a hostile sentiment to New York City, allegedly the hub of the villainry which would impose discount stores and retail chains upon consumers. Lending support to the conspiracy theory of Wall Street's promotion of mass distribution was the fact that one of the few congressmen to speak out against the Robinson-Patman Act was Emmanuel Celler of New York.

[7] Arthur M. Schlesinger, Jr. (1960), writes of the White House indifference, "New Deal liberalism [at the time] had other clients; it had not yet embarked on its unrequited love affair with small business" (p. 510).

ROBINSON–PATMAN ACT AS PRECURSOR OF REGULATORY REFORM

The Robinson–Patman Act is of interest not only as a model of New Deal legislation. It is also a precursor of the current regulatory reform movement and, thereby, informs us as to the direction of this movement. The Robinson–Patman Act is perhaps the first important piece of New Deal legislation for which those in the American liberal tradition can now respectably express their distaste. One need not hold to the economic philosophy of the Chicago School to oppose the Robinson–Patman Act. In first mounting the attack against laws regarding price discrimination and bringing about this state of affairs, the role of two economists and that of a committee must be appreciated.

M. A. Adelman (1949, 1953, 1959) was the first to expose the fallacies in the attack on secondary line price discrimination.[8] Later John S. McGee (1958), under the intellectual inspiration of Aaron Director, demonstrated the unlikelihood of predatory pricing as an effective or workable monopolizing device.[9] In the intervening years, the Attorney General's National Committee To Study the Antitrust Laws (of which Adelman was an influential member) recommended a weakening of the Robinson–Patman Act, citing the vagaries of the act's language and its enforcement.[10]

The upshot of these writings and their progeny is notable and must be surprising to anyone who questions the potential impact of an idea in print. Within the literature of economics, the current legal doctrines on price discrimination now receive hostile treatment, even in elementary textbooks.[11] To be critical of the Robinson–Patman Act has become, in Galbraith's term, a part of the "conventional wisdom" of economics. The treatment is much the same in the legal profession. One recent head (Baker, 1975) of the Antitrust Division sees, as the act's only benefit, that it " . . . provides a full employment program for antitrust law-

---

[8] Secondary line price discrimination is when anticompetitive effects from the practice occur at the level of the buyer of the discriminating firm.

[9] The literature that expanded upon McGee's work is extensive. Much of it has been reprinted in Yale Brozen (1975).

[10] See the Attorney General's National Committee To Study the Antitrust Laws (1955). In addition to this committee, and the two economists cited, honorable mention goes to an attorney, F. M. Rowe (who was a conferee of the Attorney General's Committee) for educating a generation of lawyers and law students about the complexities and incongruities of the Robinson–Patman Act. See F. M. Rowe (1962, 1964). For a contemporary survey see Erwin A. Elias (1975).

[11] In Paul Samuelson's *Economics* (1973) the act is described as " . . . antitrust legislation [that] has acted to increase monopolistic imperfection of markets rather than decrease it." Edwin Mansfield (1974) placed his discussion of the act under the topic heading: "Other Policies Designed to Restrict Competition" in his *Economics*. Not all principles of economics textbooks offer an assessment of the act.

yers and professors—and provides comic relief for law students." Two presidential study groups on antitrust indicate the bipartisan nature of the criticism, both among lawyers and economists and among Democrats and Republicans. Lyndon Johnson's appointees proposed a new statute (White House Task Force Report, 1968); Richard Nixon's designates called for a broadening of the defenses to price discrimination charges and an outright repeal of three of the act's subsections (Report of the Task Force on Productivity and Competition, 1969).

However, the most remarkable effect of this critique is found among the antitrust enforcement agencies themselves. While the Antitrust Division of the Department of Justice has never shown great enthusiasm for prosecuting discriminatory pricing practices, in recent years that agency has openly criticized the Robinson-Patman Act and proposed its sweeping revision.[12] At the Federal Trade Commission, the Robinson-Patman Act enforcement was once wrought with dedication and zeal. Witness the fact that the Robinson-Patman Act was 27-years old before the Federal Trade Commission uncovered a price cut it considered justified by the act's 2(b) meeting competition defense![13] This situation has changed dramatically.

In 1960, the Federal Trade Commission filed 144 Robinson-Patman Act complaints; the number for 1974 was only 6. In the period 1960-1963, the FTC issued 116 orders under 2(c) of the act; this compares with only 21 in the entire 1964-1975 period. In 1963, the FTC issued 225 orders under Section 2(d) of the act alone; in 1975 it issued none. The Bureau of Economics and the Bureau of Competition at this agency both have shown a "tilt" in their enforcement efforts. The political impetus for the tilt inside the FTC came from Commissioner Philip Elman, himself a product of the Justice Department. His public views and his votes as a Commissioner reflected his lack of enthusiasm for the act (Elman, 1966).

So widespread has the displeasure with the Robinson-Patman Act become that, in 1975, a special ad hoc committee of Congress was formed and held hearings to protect the act from its critics.[14] To accomplish this was no small task. The committee carefully selected its friendly witnesses,[15] sought to avoid unsym-

---

[12] U.S. Dept. of Justice (1977). The "Regulatory Reform Unit" of the Department of Justice in 1975 circulated draft legislation to the Office of Management and Budget that would significantly reduce the scope of antitrust concern with price discrimination.

[13] The case is *Continental Baking Co.*, 63 FTC 207 (1963) as reported in American Bar Association, *Antitrust Law Developments* (1975), p. 144.

[14] The Ad Hoc Subcommittee On Antitrust, The Robinson-Patman Act, and Related Matters came to be called the Gonzalez committee, after its chairman, Congressman Henry B. Gonzalez of Texas. See the three volumes of *Hearings* (1976) and the subcommittee's *Report*, 1976.

[15] Business trade groups unabashedly supportive of the Act include: Associated Retail Bakers of America, Menswear Retailers of America, National Association of Music Merchants, National Association of Retail Druggists, National Association of Retail Grocers,

pathetic ones, and drafted a final report purportedly exonerating the act of any faults. The report's attempt to apply cosmetics to the Robinson-Patman Act did not leave its wrinkles exposed as much as ignored.

As yet, no legislation has been introduced in Congress to repeal the Robinson-Patman Act. Yet significant reform of the act has taken place, not by legislative fiat, but by a transformation of the act's image among those who enforce it. Given the track record of Congress in repealing any New Deal legislation,[16] this may be the manner in which regulatory reform takes place: by the education and replacement of those charged with enforcing the legislation rather than of those who write the legislation. This is what has happened with the Robinson-Patman Act and may be the avenue of reform within the non-antitrust regulatory agencies as well.[17]

This solution to the regulation problem is not, to be sure, wholly satisfactory. Philosophically, those who prefer a government of laws and not of men will blanch at the lack of principle in securing reform in this manner. In the case of the Robinson-Patman Act, continuing reform must then hinge upon a lax (or some might say astute) enforcement of the act by the government. However, even if all undesirable economic effects of the act were currently being scotched by the Federal Trade Commission, it is not prudent to rely upon the good sense of the Commission and its staff to let a sleeping dog lie. Times change and so can the composition and direction of the agency. In addition, even an omniscient FTC cannot prevent the filing of unfortunate Robinson-Patman Act cases by the private antitrust bar.

ECONOMIC ANALYSIS AND PRICE DISCRIMINATION POLICY

A further impediment to reform of the Robinson-Patman Act is the belief within the antitrust community that, while the Robinson-Patman attempt has been unfortunate, nevertheless some form of specific price discrimination law is necessary. The roots of this belief lie partly in a misplaced perception of economic theory.

National Association of Tobacco Distributors, National Candy Wholesalers Association, National Congress of Petroleum Retailers, National Federation of Independent Business, National Food Brokers Association, National Home Furnishing Association, National Independent Dairies Association, National Liquor Stores Association, National Retail Hardware Association, National Small Business Association, National Tire Dealers and Retreaders Association, Photo Marketing Association, Retail Floorcovering Inst., Retail Jewelers of America, and the Society of American Florists.

[16] The exception is Congressional repeal of the fair trade laws in 1975. See Consumer Goods Pricing Act of 1975, 89 Stat. 801.

[17] This may be the case with airline regulation, where the internal enforcement methodology of the CAB changed due to new leadership before Congress authorized deregulation by statute.

Economic orthodoxy holds that price discrimination is a manifestation of monopoly power in which the seller segregates (at least two) customers who have different demand elasticities and charges them discriminatory prices. In so doing, the seller's profits exceed those that could be made under a nondiscriminatory pricing structure. The implications for ardent antitrusters of this analysis proved to be murky. Supporters of antiprice discrimination laws pointed to the clear tenet of orthodoxy that the existence of price discrimination was itself a sign of monopoly power and therefore any firm able to discriminate should be made to stop.

Other antitrusters argued that discriminatory pricing was an effect, not a cause, of monopoly power. Upon observing discriminatory pricing, the appropriate response was, therefore, to attack the structure of the industry rather than try to deter a firm's discriminatory pricing conduct.

The only defense offered for discriminatory pricing was that it could (depending upon the shape of the firm's demand curves) improve economic efficiency by inducing a firm to expand output beyond the single-price profit-maximizing level. This would reduce the loss in economic welfare caused by the firm's monopoly position; therefore, to prohibit price discrimination could lower the value of total output.[18]

Without gainsaying the usefulness of this analysis for some problems, the comparative statics of conventional price discrimination models actually can conceal and confuse the understanding needed for sound antitrust policy formulation in this area, because the neo-orthodox models are models of equilibrium. They show best the implications of price discrimination by a firm in a steady-state position, but the phenomenon which has elicited most Robinson–Patman Act attention is a disequilibrium situation. While price discrimination could be evidence of a profitable exploitation of a monopoly position, generally it signals a *breakdown* in market power and a movement toward a competitive equilibrium.

The move to competitive equilibrium, especially in oligopolistic markets, usually involves price discrimination. However, the discrimination that occurs in disequilibrium is not to be mistaken for the discrimination of the ensconced firm with market power. The dynamics of the discrimination are actually a hastening of the market equilibrating process that brings prices in line with costs.

The fallacy of much Robinson–Patman Act enforcement is that it represents only a snapshot of the pricing process (as does elementary price theory). This snapshot may catch prices in the act of discrimination, but a filming of the entire pricing process would reveal that the discrimination represents a movement to a new competitive equilibrium which will have a relative absence of discrimi-

---

[18] Notable modifications to this canon have been the work of Gordon Tullock (1967), Oliver E. Williamson (1974), and B. S. Yamey (1974).

nation. The pertinent characteristic about this process is that, in the absence of corrective discrimination, the equilibrating process will take longer. Can there be any doubt that if sellers had to cut prices to all of their customers everywhere in one simultaneous swoop regardless of competitive conditions, such across-the-board cuts would be slower in coming?

An understanding of price discrimination as disequilibrium, coupled with the antitrust experience and scholarship of the recent past, supports the proposition that the Sherman Act could be an adequate weapon to counter any genuinely anticompetitive discriminatory pricing practice.

A TIME FOR CHANGE

Critics of the Robinson-Patman Act can be divided into two camps. The first holds that the case-law under the act is so complicated and unworkable that businesses can circumvent the act through adroit use of private labels, vertical integration, nonprice competition, concealed discounts, astute legal advice, or simply because of the limited enforcement budget of the Federal Trade Commission. To repeal or reform the act, then, would remove an unpleasant irritation to the economic system, but the effect on consumer welfare would not be all that great. The second camp holds that the act imposes substantial economic harm upon the economy because of its anticompetitive hindrance of price cutting, new entry, and price flexibility. To this group, repeal or reform has a high priority.

The former group has the better of the argument. A comparison of the United States and Canada is revealing in this regard. Canada has no law against price discrimination comparable to that of the United States. Yet the percentage of retail trade done by single store retailers in Canada is nearly identical to the situation in the United States.[19] This is the case both overall and for two significant categories of retailing: grocery stores and drug stores. If anything, Canada has a greater proportion of such outlets. In a comparison of only the province of Ontario with the state of Michigan, the similarity continues.[20] Single outlet

[19] See U.S. Department of Justice (1977), p. 202. As a percentage of retail sales the business done by single store outlets is

	United States (1966)	Canada (1967)
Overall	60.2	61.8
Grocery Stores	38.9	41.6
Drug Stores	61.0	76.5

[20] United States Department of Justice (1977), p. 206.

stores recently had 58.2% of total sales in Ontario, 56.9% in Michigan; such stores comprised 83.9% of all outlets in Ontario, 86.7% in Michigan. The Robinson-Patman Act apparently has not been the protective measure for small business its supporters had hoped.

Indeed, it is not far fetched to conclude that the main beneficiaries of the Robinson-Patman Act are, paradoxically, oligopolistic industries, or even members of cartels. Economic theory neatly shows that in an effective cartel, each member has an incentive to cheat on the monopoly price and restricted output by cutting price and expanding shipments. To the extent a cartelist is deterred from cutting a price to a selected buyer, for fear of a Robinson-Patman Act violation, the cartel has a simpler job of maintaining internal discipline.[21] It is noteworthy that members of the Fortune 500 have not extended themselves in pushing for repeal of the Robinson-Patman Act.

Even if the efficiency impediments of the Robinson-Patman Act can be skirted and even assuming the act does not provide a secure haven for price-fixers, the costs of the act are still not *de minimus*. If only to nullify misallocative effects, a considerable amount of managerial time and legal resources must still be spent to accomplish circumvention of, or compliance with, the act. The magnitude of these costs has been estimated to be $1.4 billion for the 1936-1974 period (Elzinga and Hogarty 1978). A management occupied in concocting Robinson-Patman Act avoidance, learning the intricacies of the law, or engaged in litigation is diverted from the more socially productive tasks of management.

Two revisions are to be commended in reforming the Robinson-Patman Act if outright repeal is impossible. The first would be to remove from the statute all language concerning the protection of competitors. The appropriate focus of any price discrimination statute should be on the competitive process and the effects of such pricing on that process, not on the status of individual competitors. This is one of the commendable aspects of the reform measure suggested by the Neal Report. (White House Task Force Report, 1969).

In addition, Robinson-Patman Act enforcement illustrates the dangers of utilizing a fully allocated accounting cost standard instead of the economic concept of opportunity cost. A preferable benchmark would be the direct costs of the sales. As long as sales can be made at prices that exceed or equal marginal costs, such transactions should be allowed.[22] These sales indicate that there are individ-

---

[21] In fact, former Assistant Attorney General Thomas Kauper has testified that attorneys for companies under investigation for price-fixing have maintained that the price discussions were prompted by a desire to comply with the meeting competition defense and, in order not to give a discount to a customer exceeding that extended by a rival, in violation of the Robinson-Patman Act. See U.S. Department of Justice (1977), pp. 59-61.

[22] A potential problem may arise if prices above marginal cost are used as limit (or stayout) prices. However, such prices are still not predatory in the usual sense. Moreover, such tactics will not be effective against existing firms.

uals who value resources more highly in the production of these goods than in alternative uses; It would likely be inefficient and lessen consumer welfare to deny businesses and customers the opportunity to consummate such sales, even if the price did not equal direct costs *and* some arbitrary apportionment of the firm's already sunk fixed costs.[23]

The New Deal represented, at root, an attempt to offer assistance and economic privilege to a variety of specialized economic interests, what Ernest Griffith called "group utilitarianism." For example, the Robinson–Patman Act looks toward the interests of selected distributors. Someone well outside the New Deal camp once suggested a different course. The ardent trustbuster Henry Simons (1948) wrote that anyone may " ... see the dictates of sound policy, if he will look at every issue from the viewpoint of consumers." The Robinson–Patman Act is a violation of this precept. Simons no doubt would have agreed that the time is ripe for reform of Robinson–Patman's unfortunate attempt at the control of price differences.

ACKNOWLEDGMENT

The author is indebted to his friend and colleague William Breit for his comments on this chapter.

REFERENCES

Adelman, M. A. The A&P case: A study in applied economic theory. *Quarterly Journal of Economics*, 1949, *63*, 238.
Adelman, M. A. The consistency of the Robinson–Patman Act. *Stanford Law Review*, 1953, *6*, 3.
Adelman, M. A. *A&P: A study in cost–price behavior and public policy*. Cambridge: Harvard Univ. Press, 1959.
Attorney General's National Committee to Study the Antitrust Laws. *Report*. Washington, D.C.: United States Government Printing Office, 1955.
Baker, D. I. Robinson–Patman history and reform: From fear to futility. *Hearings on the Robinson–Patman Act* Before the Domestic Council Review Group on Regulatory Reform, Dec. 9, 1975, mimeo, p. 25.
Brozen, Y., ed. *The competitive economy: Selected readings*. Morristown: General Learning Press, 1975.
Edwards, C. D. *The price discrimination law*. Washington, D.C.: Brookings Institution, 1959.
Elias, E. A. Robinson–Patman: Time for rechiseling. *Mercer Law Review*, 1975, *26*, 689.

---

[23] A feature of "The Predatory Practices Act of 1975" is its requirement that a successful primary line discrimination case must be based on the finding of sustained selling below short-run marginal costs. Short run sales below marginal costs may result from a mistaken estimate about future revenues or costs. Even if long continued, sales below direct costs may be the equivalent of an advertising investment and pose no threat to competition.

Elman, P. The Robinson–Patman Act and Antitrust Policy: a time for reappraisal. *Washington Law Review*, 1966, *42*, 1.

Elzinga, K. G. in *Hearings*, Recent efforts to amend or repeal the Robinson–Patman Act, Committee on Small Business, House of Representatives, 94th Congress, 2nd session, Jan.-March, 1976, part 3, pp. 318-319.

Elzinga, K. G., and Hogarty, T. F. Utah Pie and the consequences of Robinson–Patman. *Journal of Law and Economics*, 1978, *22*, 427.

Hawley, E. W. *The New Deal and the problem of monopoly*. Princeton: Princeton Univ. Press, 1966.

Mansfield, E. *Economics*. New York: W. W. Norton, 1974. Pp. 531-532.

McGee, J. S. Predatory price cutting: The Standard Oil (N.J.) case. *Journal of Law and Economics*, 1958, *1*, 137.

National Dairy Products Corp., 71 FTC 1412 (1967).

Report of the Task Force on Productivity and Competition, mimeo, March, 1969, pp. 7-9, 26-27. (Reprinted in *Antitrust Law and Economics Review*, 1969, *2*, 3).

Report of the Ad Hoc Subcommittee on Antitrust, The Robinson–Patman Act, And Related Matters, Committee on Small Business, House of Representatives. House Report No. 94-1738, Washington, D.C. Sept. 1976.

Rowe, R. M. *Price discrimination under the Robinson–Patman Act*. Boston: Little, Brown, 1962.

Rowe, F. M. The federal trade commission's administration of the anti-price discrimination law—A paradox of antitrust policy. *Columbia Law Review*, 1964, *64*, 415.

Samuelson, P. *Economics*. New York: McGraw-Hill, 1973, 9th ed., p. 523.

Schlesinger, A. M., Jr. *The politics of upheaval*. Cambridge: Riverside Press, 1960.

Simons, H. *Economic policy for a free society*. Univ. of Chicago Press, 1948.

Tugwell, R. G. *Roosevelt's revolution*. New York: MacMillan, 1977.

United States Department of Justice. *Report on the Robinson–Patman Act*. Chapter 11, 1977.

Tullock, G. The welfare costs of tariffs, monopolies, and thefts. *Western Economic Journal*, 1967, *5*, 224.

White House Task Force Report on Antitrust Policy, July, 1968. [Reprinted *in BNA Antitrust and Trade Regulation Report*, No. 411, May 27, (1969).]

Williamson, O. E. The economics of antitrust: Transaction cost considerations. *University of Pennsylvania Law Review*, 1974, *122*, 1439, 1447-1449.

Yamey, B. S. Monopolistic price discrimination and economic welfare. *Journal of Law and Economics*, 1974, *17*, 377.

Discussion

VICTOR P. GOLDBERG

I agree with Elzinga that the Robinson–Patman Act is an ill-conceived and expensive nuisance. In the historical context it is easy to see why Congress felt disposed to act. The Depression was decreasing the demand faced by small businesses; unemployed laborers were becoming petty capitalists adding to the difficulties of the established retailers. Moreover, economies of mass marketing—supermarkets and chain stores—were becoming significant in the 1930s adding to the industry's woes. The act was an attempt to protect an ill-defined group (small businessmen? existing retailers and wholesalers?) from both the short-run disequilibrium problems of the Great Depression and the long-run consequences of the creative destruction process. The issue that should puzzle economists in this instance—and it seems in many other instances as well—is, why was the political solution of the shoot-the-messenger variety?

I want to take issue with Elzinga on two specific points. First, the existence of price discrimination is not confined to the two instances he discusses—monopolies segregating customer classes and oligopolies engaged in disequilibrium price competition. In a manufacturer-retailer relationship, for example, the discount structure might represent an indirect way of paying some retailers for providing extra retail services. (Clever accounting might enable us to cost-justify the discounts and remove the label, or stigma, of price discrimination.) More fundamentally, Elzinga fails to capture the ubiquity of discrimination in the real world. The frictions inherent in a reasonably competitive industry provide ample opportunity for discrimination. Restaurants can charge a high price for a cup of coffee not because they are monopolists, in any interesting sense of the word, but because the costs to the patron of separately shopping for coffee exceed the benefits. In the economist's simplified models product strategies and price structures are generally assumed away. However, if these assumptions of convenience are dropped it is clear that firms must choose on many margins—the price structure is a decision variable which can be (and is) manipulated in the pursuit of profit. Competition will reward firms which develop attractive price structures (even though these can be characterized as discriminatory) and penalize those firms that do not.

My second point concerns Elzinga's argument that policy should be concerned with the effects on the competitive process, not on the status of individual competitors and, further, that policy should be analyzed in terms of the effects on consumers. I do not take issue with the principle, but economic analysis divorced from its social and institutional context can be extremely misleading when used to interpret that principle. In a world of imperfect information, positive transactions costs, a historically determined social context, and mortal, imperfect humans the path to the bliss point, or even lesser landmarks in the world of welfare economics, is more complex than we care to admit.

Policy must be applied in a flesh-and-blood world in which people do not always follow the rules or take the rules as immutable; moreover, they have notions of what behavior or institutions are fair or legitimate and these conceptions will influence their behavior and, consequently, social outcomes. To illustrate the point I will use a dramatically simplified example. Assume that we are in a world in which utility is measurable in dollars. Assume further that if manufacturer-retailer relationships were determined solely by private contract, the optimal contracts would have all dealers subject to immediate termination regardless of cause. If dealers abide by these contracts, then GNP—total utility— would be $100 billion. Suppose, however, that dealers feel that bad faith termination is wrong or unfair—even though they had accepted it in the initial contract—and that such terminations trigger a response of imposing costs (on the manufacturer, society at large, or even themselves). The costs can take the form of violent, destructive behavior, increased political activity, and so forth. As a consequence, GNP is only $80 billion (by hypothesis). If now, we were to impose on this world a law prohibiting bad faith dealer termination, we will find that this impairs technical efficiency (incompetent dealers are more likely to survive), but that the cost-imposing response is less likely to be triggered; GNP in this instance is $90 billion. The economist generally poses the issue as outcome one versus three and, not surprisingly, opts for the former (which, alas, yields outcome two). A proper application of the consumer welfare criterion, however, would tell us to accept the policy which "protected competitors," since such protection has, by hypothesis, an indirect influence on total output.

The example is, of course, extremely artificial, but the point is real. Policy must take into account extant notions of fairness and legitimacy while recognizing existing and emerging power. Policy makers may still attempt to influence these elements, blocking recognition of some "right" and accelerating the acceptance of others, but the range of choice is constrained by the socio-institutional setting. The art of policy making is to discern the boundaries within which discretion can be exercised and to influence the drift of those boundaries over time.

I do not, I hasten to add, contend that this broadened perspective invalidates Elzinga's conclusions concerning the Robinson-Patman Act. My criticism is aimed at his general comment, not his specific application. My own expectation is that the Robinson-Patman Act's decline will continue whether or not Congress repeals it. I also expect that the application of antitrust law to vertical relationships will follow the path of the employment relationship with increased collective bargaining and job (dealer) security. But that is another story.

Chapter 5

Banking Reform in the 1930s

HOMER JONES

INTRODUCTION

One of the most visible and major aspects of the early years of the Great Depression was the waves of bank failures. These followed similar widespread failures in the 1920s, mostly in the agricultural regions. Accordingly, as the Depression continued, proposals for banking reform increased, and some actions were taken, especially in 1933 and 1935.

Several of the monetary actions and events, though dramatic and important at the time, shall not be discussed here because of limited space and because they are not as important to our problems today. Notable actions of the Great Depression years that shall not be considered here are the devaluation of the dollar, the inflow of gold, and the gold and silver purchase programs.

THE 1933–1935 REFORMS

The primary actions to be considered are: (*a*) changes in the structure and powers of the Federal Reserve System, (*b*) control of the interest paid by banks on deposits, (c) more rigid control of the establishment of banks, (d) more exacting bank examination and supervision, and finally (e) federal insurance of bank deposits.

Federal Reserve Structure

The Federal Reserve Board became the Board of Governors of the Federal Reserve System in 1933 and the Secretary of the Treasury and the Comptroller of the Currency were no longer members. In light of more than 40 years of experience, this change appears to have been cosmetic and of no great significance, although some might argue that, without this change, we would have an even worse record of financing government deficits through the creation of money.

The most notable change in structure was the establishment of the Federal Open Market Committee (FOMC). This consisted of the Board of Governors and five Federal Reserve Bank presidents. The FOMC superseded the Open Market Policy Conference, which had consisted of a representative from each Reserve bank and had operated since March 1930. While the FOMC may not have functioned with distinction in its more than 40 years of existence, it has surely been an improvement over the disastrous Open Market Conference. The advantage of the FOMC has been its guidance by somewhat more enlightened principles regarding the financial system as a whole. However, its record has been inferior to that of the Open Market Investment Committee (OMIC) which operated from 1922 through 1929. OMIC consisted of five Federal Reserve Bank presidents, with New York's president holding the chairmanship.

Powers of the Federal Reserve

The legislation of 1933-1935 increased the power and flexibility of the Federal Reserve in several respects. The system could make loans to member banks with greater flexibility, and the backing for Federal Reserve notes and deposits became less rigid. If the system had wished to operate with greater flexibility before 1933, it probably could have always obtained the needed powers from Congress. However, in any case, it would never again even appear to be inhibited legally from meeting the requirements of the monetary system.

Reserve Requirements. The Federal Reserve Board was empowered in 1933 and 1935 to alter reserve requirements. The original rationale for this congressional grant of power, or the advantage it could have had over open market operations is not clear, but the use of this power, as we shall see below, became important in 1936-1937.

Demand Deposit Interest. An important provision of the 1933–1935 legislation, which had been long desired by major elements of the banking industry, was the prohibition of interest on demand deposits. In connection with the 1930–1933 crisis, some argued that the banking system had been seriously weakened by competitive payments of interest on demand deposits. Many believed that the practice had harmfully drained funds from the country districts into the speculative security markets. Later research, however, has not shown harmful results from interest on demand deposits in pre-1933 periods. The restrictive action that removed interest on demand deposits was a result of the same philosophy that gave us the National Recovery Administration (NRA). The difference was that the NRA was declared unconstitutional while the banking acts were not. Though dormant earlier, banking act provisions have plagued us in recent decades, as will be shown.

Interest on Time Deposits. Similar to the prohibition of interest on demand deposits, was the new power to set maximum interest on time deposits. This, too, was based on misapprehensions concerning the causes of the Great Depression, and on the long-standing direction of the banks toward cartelization and restraint of trade. As it happened, the maxima that were established were well above the market interest rates of the time. Interest rate control remained a dead letter for decades, and came into its own to plague the banking and monetary system only long after World War II.

Control of Establishment of Banks

Out of the bank failures of 1921–1933, and the general financial and economic debacle of 1930–1933, arose a belief that we had experienced widespread over-banking in the country. However, given our propensity for a unit banking system and given the transportation technology of pre-World War I, we were not over-supplied with banks in 1920. With the introduction of the automobile as local transportation, some of the banks became redundant. However, if the philosophy of the day had permitted the Federal Reserve to lend to banks on a basis of their long-term prospects, either for continued operation, or for orderly liquidation, we need not have had the waves of bank failures.

After all, we did have the failures and, in 1933–1935, the opinion was widespread that too much freedom in the establishment of banks had been a major cause of our troubles. Supporting this was the cartel-restraint-of-competition attitude of the time. Consequently, in the 1930s, a century of freedom in chartering of banks was at an end, and a bank could henceforth be established only if government officials could be persuaded that it was necessary to meet the "convenience and needs of the community." This new restraint-of-trade power was probably inimical to the recovery in the 1930s, and current day investigators are now convinced that it has become increasingly harmful in recent decades.

Bank Supervision

Government examination and supervision of banks received renewed impetus and vigor as a result of the Great Depression. It was widely felt that the supervisors, by not being sufficiently rigorous, had contributed to the bank failures of the 1920s and the early 1930s. This was probably not the case. More likely, the examinations, through ill-timed and ill-applied controls, contributed to bank failures and to depression in general.

However, accompanying this misconception regarding the past role of examiners was an additional new examining force—the Federal Deposit Insurance Corporation (FDIC) examiners, who harassed the shell-shocked bankers. Belief that examiners had been delinquent, and their larger numbers and greater resolve to be more restraining in the future, contributed importantly to the failure of the economy to recover more satisfactorily in 1934-1940. However, it was not until well after World War II that scholars generally began to see the harmful effects of the examination process.

Deposit Guarantee

Possibly the major banking and monetary reform, following the 1930-1933 collapse, was the adoption of federal insurance or the guarantee of bank deposits. In the following nearly half-century, there has been scarcely a word of criticism regarding this institutional change; but I shall express some reservations about the wisdom of deposit insurance, while recognizing that it would be quixotic to suggest turning back the clock.

The preferable alternatives to deposit insurance would have been, first, that the Federal Reserve should not permit any substantial, prolonged reduction in the circulating medium and, second, that the Federal Reserve should lend to meet the liquidity problems of any sound commercial bank.

It might be argued that the Federal Reserve has, in fact, operated in such a manner that deposit insurance has been unnecessary. However, the record is not reassuring.

The term "deposit insurance" has been a euphemism for deposit guarantee by the federal government. The ostensible limited coverage has, in practice, proved to be a 100% guarantee, and these guarantees have also been applied to the deposits of the savings and loan associations. So the deposits of the banks and those of the savings and loan associations both have been, and are, in effect, liabilities of the federal government. This has substantially removed surveillance by bank customers of the soundness of operation and capital structure of these financial institutions. As a result, the capital ratio of the commercial banks has declined steadily over the years.

I am suggesting that, with the lender of last resort standing ready to supply liquidity, depositor surveillance together with some limited failures of financial institutions and some accompanying minor losses to depositors, would be a very good combination, just as it was in the century of greatest economic progress preceding World War I.

Selective Credit Controls

Selective credit controls were an integral part of the financial reforms of the Roosevelt era. The great growth of consumer credit in the 1920s was widely believed to have been "unsound" and to have contributed substantially to the 1929-1933 collapse. Similarly, lenient housing and other mortgage credit terms were believed to have been unsound and to have contributed to economic collapse. These matters were the subject of extensive, organized research by many economists in the 1920s and the 1930s and, as is usual when economists investigate an alleged problem, it was generally found that something should be done. This recommendation was ready for adoption in World War II, just when production of durable consumer goods and houses was curtailed anyway. Control of the terms of consumer credit lending was impractical to administer, despite an army of enforcers. This adverse experience with such controls did not prevent their reflexive adoption again in the Korean War, with similar results. Today,[1] we have again provided the president with the power to reimpose such selective controls, as discussed extensively by Hodgman (1972).

STATISTICAL BEHAVIOR OF THE MONEY STOCK 1919-1976

Let us look briefly at the behavior of the economy, and of banking, as well as the monetary aggregates in the post-World War I period. Then we can compare the behavior of the economy and of money, after World War II, when these factors were influenced by the rule changes of the 1930s.

It is generally agreed that the economic system worked better in the 22 years (1945-1967), following World War II, than it did in the preceding 22 years (1918-1940); and that, on the whole, this better experience has continued up to the present.[2] We probably cannot agree on why the later experience has been better than the earlier one, or on the prospects now for the future. However, I

[1] Credit Control Act (Public Law 91-151, 91st Congress Sec. 2577, Title II) that became law December 23, 1969.
[2] Brookings Institution, 1978-I, pp. 14, 16, 47, 48, 51, 53.

TABLE 5.1
Mean and Standard Deviation of Rates of Change of the Money Supply, Wholesale Prices and Real GNP[a]

	M1		M2		WP		Real GNP	
	Mean	SD	Mean	SD	Mean	SD	Mean	SD
1919-1929	3.23	6.17	5.27	5.87	−1.96	12.52	2.61	7.25
1919-1933	.52	7.19	1.53	8.52	−3.73	11.50	−.28	8.21
1929-1939	2.83	9.77	.97	9.27	−1.68	8.86	1.09	8.91
1919-1939	3.14	8.16	3.26	8.05	−1.83	10.85	1.63	8.09
1946-1956	2.89	2.32	3.57	2.51	5.02	8.37	1.84	6.48
1956-1966	2.43	1.62	4.95	2.33	1.17	1.44	3.76	2.16
1946-1966	2.73	1.99	4.38	2.46	3.09	6.34	2.84	4.93
1966-1976	5.61	1.34	8.43	2.03	6.11	5.48	2.99	2.87
1946-1976	3.69	2.29	5.71	3.03	—	—	—	—

[a]The money supply calculations for the 1919-1939 period are based on annual data computed from figures for 1 day a month and are to be found in Friedman and Schwartz, *Monetary history of the United States.* Those for 1946-1976 are based on annual data calculated from every banking day in the year. While the use of only one observation per month in the one case, and 20 or 25 in the other makes the figures not strictly comparable, this observer believes that the calculated annual data on either basis approximates the truth closely enough to make the above comparisons reasonable and useful.

shall try to consider the significance of those changes of the thirties on the post-World War II experience. Looking at the behavior of the money supply measure, we find that it was far less erratic in the post-World War II period than in the post-World War I period. We did not have a monetary explosion in 1946 comparable to 1919, nor a destruction of money as in 1920-1921, nor collapses like those of 1930-1933 and 1936-1937. Along with the less erratic performance of money after World War II, we have seen more stability in the growth of real GNP and in the behavior of wholesale prices. (See Table 5.1).

THE LAST TWENTY YEARS—THE 1933-1935 REFORMS IN PERSPECTIVE

Investigations and Literature

Dissatisfaction with the structure and operations of the monetary and financial systems has been widespread, and has resulted in numerous formal investigations, much scholarly thought and research, and a great, independent literature. Among the formal investigations have been the Commission on Money and Credit of 1958-1961, the Heller Committee of 1962-1963, the Hunt Commission of 1970-1971, and the congressional studies of 1975-1976, commonly referred to as FINE. Among the independent studies have been those of Haywood (1976), Benston (1972), and Cox (1966). By and large, these investigations have come to naught. The defects that they have found in the reforms of 1933-1935 have become the status quo and difficult or impossible to change.

Reserve Requirements

In August 1936, and March and May 1937, reserve requirements were doubled within a 9 month period. This was the principal occasion that the power to control reserve requirements has ever been used in any substantial way. When that crude instrument was used, the rate of increase of money (M1) fell from a 16% rate, in the period of March 1932 to March 1936, to a 7% increase rate, and then turned into a declining rate in the period from January 1937 to February 1938.

In the 1933-1936 period, bank reserves, bank credit, and the money supply had increased rapidly, thanks primarily to a great inflow of gold rather than to the Federal Reserve. The gold inflow was used in three ways: (*a*) banking and monetary expansion, (*b*) sterilization by the Treasury, and (*c*) growth of reserves, particularly excess reserves of the commercial banks.

Seen in historical perspective, the resulting excess reserves were desirable to the banks, especially in light of the traumatic experience of 1930-1933. The advance in the total amount of reserves was necessary in order to expand the amount of credit and monetary expansion. If the "excess" reserves had not been available, the banks would not have re-expanded as they did. If we had not received the fortuitous inflow of gold, and had been dependent on the Federal Reserve to create the volume of reserves, we would have been disappointed; bank expansion, money volume, and economic recovery would have been less than they were in 1933-1936. The Federal Reserve authorities of the day did not see that the total reserves and the excess reserves were necessary to accomplish the economic expansion that we experienced in 1933-1936.

When the reserve requirements were raised and the excess reserves thereby destroyed in August 1936, a great reduction in the rate of increase of money quickly followed. When reserve requirements were further increased in the spring of 1937, the slackening increase of money quickly became a decline. Thus, the new tool of monetary management played a major role in the economic debacle of 1936-1938, and it aborted recovery from the Great Depression.

Interest Rate Control

There has been general agreement in the last 20 years that the prohibition of interest on demand deposits, and control of interest on time deposits, have been harmful and should be repealed (Benston, 1964, 1972; Chandler and Jaffee, 1977; Chase, 1976; Cox, 1966; Friedman, 1959, 1976; Hester, 1977; Phillips, 1977, Pierce, 1977; Saving, 1972; Tobin, 1966, 1970).

Of course, if the control of the money supply is important, then so is the prohibition of interest on demand deposits and the control of interest on time deposits. Such controls have been most nefarious, and have created greater and greater difficulties. The prohibition and controls have provided a new impetus to rising velocity in times of rising interest rates, the very time when restraint is most important (Cox, 1966; Friedman, 1959, 1976, among others). Almarin Phillips (1977) has argued that, with the rapid development of electronic funds transfer, bank deposits are rapidly becoming more and more unpredictable and uncontrollable. He suggests that demand deposits, negotiable orders for withdrawal (NOW) accounts, and savings deposits should all bear interest, depending on market conditions. Almost all recent students of the problem have concluded that it was a mistake in 1935 to prohibit interest on demand deposits and to provide for control of interest on savings and time deposits.

The prohibition of interest on demand deposits results in numerous new devices such as the NOW accounts that confuse the measurement of money and the problem of control. Limitation of interest rates on loans charged by banks also adds to the problems of precision in monetary control. In times of high interest rates and high borrowing, banks must tend to increase required compensating balances, creating a distortion in, and obscuring the meaning of the quantity of money.

Interest on Interbank Deposits. Interest has never been paid on deposits of member banks in the Federal Reserve and, since 1935, has also been prohibited on interbank time deposits. It now is clear that the operations of the monetary and banking system would be greatly improved if the Federal Reserve were to pay interest on deposits, possibly at a rate fixed slightly below the market rate on 90-day Treasury bills. This would remove one of the main objections that banks have to membership and to keeping deposits in the Federal Reserve. It would also stabilize the volatility of the major element of the money stock, and thereby, remove a major threat to the monetary system.[3]

Time Deposits. Government control of the interest rates paid by banks and savings associations on time and savings accounts, has proven to be an important defect of the monetary system in the past 2 decades. These controls have made for cyclical disintermediation and reintermediation to the detriment of the banks, the savings associations, their depositors, and their borrowers. The detrimental effects have been demonstrated by a host of scholars and investigations

---

[3] Note: Chairman Miller was reported in *Business Week,* May 8, 1978, p. 37 as proposing that the Federal Reserve should pay interest on bank deposits.

(e.g., Benston, 1964; Cox, 1966; FINE, 1976; Friedman, 1959, 1976; Haywood, 1968; Luttrell, 1968; Ruebling, 1970; and earlier formal studies). There has been a general conclusion that the provision for such controls in the 1930s has proven to be a major error. However, as with many other provisions of law rather thoughtlessly enacted in the 1930s, this control has proven an ineradicable incubus. Some of those in the housing industry think that interest-rate control is to their advantage, whereas it probably increases the cyclical nature of the housing industry, with a scarcity of funds and with higher interest rates than might otherwise exist in the upward phase of the cycle. The problems arising from this situation tend to be met by complex rules and regulations.

The controls are exercised by numerous agencies that are now pledged not to change rules unless all act in concert. Thus, these controls add increasingly to the inefficiencies in the financial system. Although it is of great urgency that the control of interest rates be eliminated, there appears little chance that this will take place.

Establishment and Entry

Rigid control of the establishment of new banks has continued to this day. The policy was most notably violated by the Comptroller of the Currency in the liberal chartering of national banks in the 1960s. However, in the main, the chartering of banks and admission to deposit insurance have been directed, since the 1930s, by the immediate interests of the existing banks and not of the depositing and borrowing public.

Most scholars who have recently studied the control in establishing new banks have concluded that the economy would benefit greatly by substantial reversion to the free banking system (e.g., Chandler and Jaffee, 1977; Pelzman, 1965, 1969, 1970, 1974). It is fair to note, however, that these same scholars generally favor a free-market economic system. My own experience leads me to conclude that we have suffered from bureaucratic control of the establishment of banks and that the public interest would benefit from reconsidering elements of the free banking system.

Supervision, Regulation, and Examination

Most recent students investigating government supervision of banks agree that government supervision of the banks has been extremely harmful to efficient, socially useful, commercial bank operations (e.g., Benston, 1974; Chase, 1976; Friedman, 1976; Scott, 1975). These investigators have found that such supervision, particularly the control of the character of bank assets, has been increasingly conducive to economic fluctuations and to misallocations of credit.

Government supervision of the banks is closely related to deposit insurance and to the relative decline of bank capital. It is widely suggested that, if private investors would put more capital into banks, relative to total assets or to risk assets, supervision could be less onerous and the allocation of funds left much more to the marketplace (e.g., Chase, 1976). A major suggestion has been that the deposit insurance premium rates should be reduced as capital ratios increase.

The reforms of 1933–1935 did little to centralize bank supervision. Indeed, with the establishment of Federal Deposit Insurance, supervision became more multifaceted than ever before. Some students feel that this has been beneficial, thinking that only thereby has some element of free private initiative been retained in the banking system (Friedman, 1976). Others have felt that the multiplicity of supervisors has competitively prevented enforcement of capital ratio requirements and, thereby, necessitated continued and increased supervision of operations.

Deposit Insurance

Deposit insurance has generally been regarded as a bright star in the firmament of New Deal legislation. It has been praised for preventing runs on banks and, thereby, for contributing to the stability of the economic system and avoiding waves of destruction of the circulating medium. However, in recent years, the system has been found to have serious defects. The uniform rates of assessment are believed to provide a motive for bankers to minimize their capital investment, and to deprive them of a strong motive for evaluating the risks of their operation and responding accordingly (Benston, 1974; Dwyer, 1978; Pelzman, 1974; Schwartz, 1975). A proposed palliative for this difficulty is that the rates of assessment upon the insured banks (and possibly savings and loan associations as well) should be graduated according to the degree of risk evidenced by each insured institution. This degree of risk would be determined by the government examiners.[4]

The most promising basis for determining a premium related to risk would be the capital ratio of the institution. This would be a crude but somewhat meaningful basis for determining rates. The greater the capital ratio, the greater the risk born by the stockholders and the less the risk born by the insurer and thus, the less the assessment or premium.

I can think of no better criterion that would conceivably work (Benston, 1974). A very common basis of bank failure is fraud, but I think we can scarcely visualize examiners estimating the chance of fraud, much less making their estimates known, and levying assessments on the basis of their judgments. Examiners now isolate some assets of banks that they consider to bear substantial

---

[4] I should not object to this recommendation on the grounds that it is politically unfeasible (nothing has happened in the years since it was first proposed) because my suggestion has probably even less chance of favorable reception.

chance of loss. Conceivably, the greater the proportion of assets in high risk categories, the greater could be the assessment rate, but the record of successful anticipation of losses by the examiners has not been very good. Further, by the time an asset is classified, the banker is already motivated to try to avoid loss.

The ideal way to avoid the baleful effects of deposit insurance would be to eliminate the institution. I do not doubt that this suggestion is quixotic, but, if so, I am not able to distinguish between this and the other financial reforms that are suggested, year after year, and that make no progress. In my view, we would never have needed federal guarantee of the liabilities of financial institutions if the Federal Reserve had not contracted the money supply, if the bank examiners had valued bank assets on a basis of their estimated long-run payout value, and if the Federal Reserve had been able to make loans on that basis. So, for the future, if the Federal Reserve would refrain from contraction and would lend upon a basis of long-term prospects, and if the examiners would value on a basis of long-term prospects, we could eliminate deposit insurance and its deleterious side effects.

CONCLUSIONS

We have observed that the monetary banking system worked better after World War II than after World War I, but was this due to the reforms of 1933-1935? I think that some of the reforms have been beneficial, some have had mixed effects, and some have been very harmful.

The changes in structure, powers, and principles of the Federal Reserve may be considered helpful in preventing a recurrence of the debacles of 1920-1922 and 1929-1933. On the other hand, they may have contributed to the secular inflation which has plagued us in recent years.

Deposit insurance is almost universally acclaimed, but, as I have noted, most recent students have found that its existence contributes importantly to current problems. I believe that, if the Federal Reserve were encouraged to lend liberally to banks under stress, and if examiners valued assets less stringently in times of stress, deposit insurance would be unnecessary.

We have seen that, for whatever reasons and whatever the connection between them, both the economic system and the monetary system have, on the whole, done much better in the period 1946-1977 than in 1919-1940. However, there is widespread testimony that existing monetary and banking rules, regulations and other "requirements" are leading to crisis in our current system. The most serious of these would seem to be, first, the prohibition and controls of interest rates on the deposits of banks and other financial institutions, and the failure of the Federal Reserve to pay interest on reserves, and, second, an implicit requirement that the Federal Reserve validate increases in the wage level.

In this connection, the most important reversal of the mistakes of 1933-1935 would be the repeal of prohibition of interest payments on demand deposits, the abandonment of interest ceilings on time and savings deposits, and the payment of interest on bank deposits at the Federal Reserve. This has been the testimony of most objective observers who have studied the subject in the last 2 decades.

These suggestions may be just as quixotic as the suggestions that deposit insurance be phased out.[5] Financial institutions think that, on the whole, they would be harmed by a repeal of the prohibition and controls on interest rates. The housing interests do not recognize that they would be benefited, not harmed, and that the housing cycle would be greatly ameliorated. Consumer advocates do not recognize that controlled interest rates on deposits have scarcely kept up with inflation, so that the common person has been receiving close to a zero interest rate on deposits.

REFERENCES

Benston, G. J. Interest payments on demand deposits and bank investment behavior. *Journal of Political Economy*, 1964, *72*, 431-449.

Benston G. J. Discussion of the Report of the President's Commission on Financial Structure and Regulation. (Hunt Commission Report). *Journal of Money, Credit, and Banking*, 1972, *4*, 985-989.

Benston, G. J., and Marlin, J. T. Bank examiners' evaluation of credit. *Journal Money, Credit, and Banking*, 1974, *6*, 23-44.

Brookings Institution. *Economic Activity, 1978-I*. Washington, D.C., 1978.

Chandler, L. V., and Jaffee, D. M. A review of the FINE regulatory reforms. *Journal of Money, Credit, and Banking*, 1977, *9*, 619-635.

Chase, S. B. The structure of federal regulation of depository institutions. In *FINE - Compendium of papers*. Bk. I. pp. 145-171, 94th Cong., 2d sess., June, 1976.

Commission on Money and Credit. Issued seventeen volumes of studies, etc. New York: Prentice-Hall. (CMC), 1958-1961.

Commission on Financial Structure and Regulation. *The Report of the President's Commission on Financial Structure and Regulation*. Washington, D.C.: United States Government Printing Office (Hunt Commission), 1971.

Committee on Financial Institutions. *Report to the President of the United States*. Washington D.C.: United States Government Printing Office. (Heller Report), 1963.

Cox, A. H., Jr. *Regulation of Interest Rates on Bank Deposits*. Ann Arbor, Mich.: University of Michigan, Bureau of Business Research, 1966.

Dwyer, G. P., Jr. The effects of the banking acts of 1933 and 1935 on capital investment in commercial banking. Unpublished manuscript, 1978.

FINE. Financial Institutions and the Nation's Economy. (The FINE Study). For complete citations see U.S. Congress. House.

---

[5] For an admirable, succinct statement of the reasons that the mistaken financial legislation of 1933 is now ineradicably embedded in the economic system, see Pierce (1977), especially pp. 616-617.

Friedman, M. *A program for monetary stability.* New York City: Fordham University Press, 1959.
Friedman, M. Testimony at *Hearings* on FINE *Discussion principles*, 1976. Pt. 3, pp. 2151-2192. Also see Pt. 4, Appendix A, pp. 231-236.
Friedman, M., & Schwartz, A. J. *Monetary history of the United States.* Princeton: Princeton University Press, 1963.
Haywood, C. F. Testimony at *Hearings* on FINE *Discussion principles*, 1975. Pt. 2, pp. 1471-1476.
Haywood, C. *Regulation Q and Monetary Policy.* Chicago: Association of Reserve City Bankers, 1971.
Hester, D. D. Special interests: the FINE situation. *Journal of Money, Credit, and Banking*, 1977, *9*, 652-661.
Hodgman, D. R. Selective credit controls. *Journal of Money, Credit, and Banking*, 1972, *4*, 342-359.
Luttrell, C. Interest rate controls: perspective, purpose and problems. Federal Reserve Bank of St. Louis, *Review*, Sept. 1968.
Mayer, T. The structure and operations of the Federal Reserve System: some needed reforms. In *FINE — Compendium of papers*, 1976, Bk. II, pp. 669-725.
Meltzer, A. What the commission didn't recommend. *Journal of Money, Credit, and Banking*, 1972, *4*, 1005-1009.
Meltzer, A. Statement at *Hearings* on FINE *Discussion principles*, 1975. Pt. 1, pp. 79-110.
Pelzman, S. Entry in commercial banking. *Journal of Law and Economics*, 1965, *8*, 11-50.
Pelzman, S. Capital investment in commercial banking and its relationship to portfolio regulation. *Journal of Political Economy*, 1970, *78*, 1-26.
Pelzman, S. The costs of competition: an appraisal of the Hunt Commission Report. *Journal of Money, Credit, and Banking*, 1972, *4*, 1001-1004.
Phillips, A. CMC, Heller, FIA, FRA, and FINE. *Journal of Money, Credit, and Banking*, 1977, *9*, 636-641.
Pierce, J. The FINE study. *Journal of Money, Credit, and Banking*, 1977, *4*, 605-618.
Robertson, R. M. *The Comptroller and Bank Supervision: A Historical Appraisal.* Washington, D.C.: The Office of the Comptroller of the Currency, 1968.
Ruebling, C. E. The administration of regulation Q. Federal Reserve Bank of St. Louis, *Review.* Feb. 1970, 29-40.
Saving, T. R. Toward a competitive financial sector. *Journal of Money, Credit, and Banking*, 1972, *4*, 897-914.
Smith, W. L. The instruments of general monetary control. *National Banking Review*, 1963a, *I*, 47-76.
Smith, W. L. Reserve requirements in the American monetary system. *Monetary Management.* New York: Prentice Hall, for the Commission on Money and Credit. pp. 175-315, 1963b.
Schwarz, A. J., Monetary trends in the U.S. and the U.K., 1878-1970. *Journal of Economic History*, 1975, *35*, 138-159.
Stein, H. The financial structure. *American Economic Review*, 1958, *48*, 64-75.
Tobin, J. Toward improving the efficiency of the monetary mechanism. *Review of Economics and Statistics*, 1966, *42*, 276-279.
Tobin, J. Deposit interest ceilings as a monetary control. *Journal of Money, Credit, and Banking*, 1970, *2*, 1-14.
U.S. Congress. House. Committee on Banking, Currency and Housing. *Financial Institutions and the Nation's Economy. Compendium of papers prepared for the FINE Study.* Book

I, Pt. 1, Pt. 2, Book II, Pt. 3, Pt. 4. 94th Cong. 2d sess., June 1976. [Book I includes a reprinting as pp. 1-24 of Financial Institutions and the Nation's Economy (FINE) *Discussion Principles*. 94th Cong. 1st sess., Nov. 1975.]

U.S. Congress. House. *Hearings on FINE Discussion Principles* before the Subcommittee on Financial Institutions, Supervision, Regulation, and Insurance of the Committee on Banking, Currency, and Housing. 94th Cong. 1st and 2d. sess. Dec. 1975-Jan. 1976.

U.S. Congress. House. *Hearings on the Financial Reform Act of 1976* before the Subcommittee on Financial Institutions, Supervision, Regulation, and Insurance of the Committee on Banking Currency, and Housing. 94th Cong., 2d. sess. Pt. 1, Pt. 2. March, 1976.

Discussion

ANNA J. SCHWARTZ

Homer Jones, in a recent letter to me, noted "that what one says about 'Roosevelt years' legislation depends considerably on one's views about 1929-1933." I agree completely. The banking reforms of the Roosevelt years were embodied in the Banking Acts of 1933 and 1935 and in the Securities Exchange Act of 1934, that dealt both with the structure and operations of commercial and savings banks and with the structure and powers of the Federal Reserve System. The reforms were intended to address what were perceived to be problems in these areas. We can ask, looking backward, whether the problems were correctly perceived. We can also look forward and ask what has been the legacy to this date of the solutions adopted.

I shall comment on Homer's discussion of three changes with respect to commercial and savings banks that were introduced during the New Deal period: (*a*) the establishment of deposit insurance, (*b*) the regulation of interest on bank deposits, and (*c*) the restrictions on multi-function commercial banking. With respect to the Federal Reserve System, I shall comment on his discussion of the following changes the New Deal legislation introduced: (*a*) the consolidation of power within the system away from the Reserve Banks and toward the Board of Governors in Washington, (*b*) the power to alter reserve requirements and (*c*) increments to the power to regulate credit.

CHANGES FOR COMMERCIAL AND SAVINGS BANKS

Establishment of Deposit Insurance

The most far-reaching change in the commercial and savings bank structure during the New Deal period was the establishment of deposit insurance as a temporary measure in the Banking Act of 1933 and as a permanent system under the provision of Title I of the Banking Act of 1935. Introduced without the support of the Roosevelt administration, though that administration later claimed credit for the reform, deposit insurance was clearly a response to the banking failures of the 1920s and 1929-1933. Given that nearly 15,000 banks had failed over the period, Congress rightly did not regard the Federal Reserve System as a bulwark against the destruction of the money supply that was entailed by bank failures. Federal deposit insurance has been accompanied by a dramatic change in commercial bank failures and in losses borne by depositors. Since a ceiling on coverage of deposits exists, reimbursement of depositors is something less than 100%, in the event of failure, but the scourge of banking panics has effectively been eliminated from the American economy.

I, therefore, do not share Homer's view that it would be desirable to eliminate deposit insurance. He says that one of the side effects of deposit insurance has been to minimize the incentive for banks to maintain high capital ratio levels and to evaluate correctly the risks of their operations. What bothers him is that "bad banks" do not go broke, no matter how badly they are managed. Instead, they are reorganized under new management or merged with a good bank, with the Federal Deposit Insurance Corporation (FDIC) assuming responsibility for losses in connection with depreciated assets. Homer would sanction bank failures and losses to depositors if the bank's operations and capital structure were unsound. As a substitute for deposit insurance, he would rely on the Federal Reserve to supply liquidity and on depositor surveillance to keep only sound banks in operation.

Neither of these proposals seems, to me, desirable as a way of preserving the positive contribution of deposit insurance and of dealing with the negative side effect. We can, however, subject banks to a market test and still protect depositors if the market's judgment is unfavorable. In recent years, the FDIC has been unwilling to permit outright failure of large banks because of the magnitude of the payout to depositors from the insurance fund that would have been required. Instead, it has arranged for bank mergers, sometimes involving a protracted period of negotiations because of the size of the failing institution. In the interim, suspicions about the soundness of the bank have diminished the going concern value of the bank to purchasers and have induced massive loans from the Federal Reserve to keep the bank afloat until completion of the merger negotiations. In effect, the FDIC has insured all short-term liabilities of insured banks.

I regard deposit insurance as indispensable to the stability of our economy, but I believe that, so long as depositors are insured, the FDIC should not shrink from closing any bank, whether small or large, if the bank's operations fail to meet a market test. In that event, uninsured creditors would face a threat of loss. The magnitude of the payout from the insurance funds should not be the criterion for determining whether to shut down a bank. To provide adequate insurance fund resources for dealing with bank failures, the FDIC could be given an unlimited claim on the Treasury.

Accordingly, unlike Homer, I rate deposit insurance as a beneficial legacy of the New Deal period.

One alternative to federal deposit insurance that Homer might have discussed is private provision of deposit insurance. No attempt was made in the 1920s by private organizations to provide such insurance. In principle, however, there seems to be no reason that private insurers should not be able to offer depositors precisely the guarantees now offered by the FDIC. Private insurers could assess insured institutions upon a graduated basis related to the degree of risk of their assets and to the adequacy of their capital structure as determined by the insurer's agents.

Regulation of Interest on Deposits

The other notable change introduced by the two banking acts of 1933 and 1935 was that banks were prohibited by law or regulation from paying interest on demand deposits and from paying interest on time deposits at rates higher than those specified by the Board of Governors for member banks and by the FDIC for insured nonmember banks.

The prohibition of payment of interest on demand deposits was a hasty and thoughtless addition to the reform package. It also reflected a judgment that the banking problems of the early 1930s derived in considerable measure from risky ventures banks took to earn enough to pay interest on demand deposits. However, the incentive for banks to use assets to yield the largest return, as judged by the banks, is in no way altered by whether or not interest is paid on demand deposits. Indeed, there is no historical evidence that the payment of interest on demand deposits increased the fraction of risky high-yield assets in bank portfolios. The prohibition was simply a government-enforced price-fixing agreement. In practice, it has been undermined by competitive banks offering "free" service to depositors in lieu of interest payments.

Over the past 6 years, Congress has been debating whether to legalize interest-bearing checking accounts. In 1973, it legalized negotiable orders for withdrawal (NOW) accounts in banks in Massachusetts and New Hampshire to permit writing of checks against interest-bearing savings accounts. A bill to authorize nationwide NOW accounts is before Congress, and has won Federal Reserve support. Arthur Burns noted

> The simple fact is that by one means or another depositors have been increasingly successful in earning interest or its equivalent on their transactions balances. Such interest is implicit in the banking services that are provided bank customers without charge or below cost . . . Congressional inaction will not stop the spread of interest payments on what are in effect transactions balances . . . (September 12, 1977).

This is a remarkable admission by the administrator of the legal prohibition of the payment of interest on demand deposits that the market has outwitted the regulators.

Another bill, that the Federal Reserve is apparently also willing to support, would make interest-bearing checking accounts legal for all kinds of financial institutions. Commercial banks, however, are fearful of the effect of direct interest payments on earnings, while savings and loan institutions, outside of the Northeast, oppose a change that appears to give commercial banks a competitive advantage. Congressional inaction reflects these special interests. The Federal Reserve has recently adopted a *regulatory* change, in order to bypass Congress, that would permit commercial banks to prearrange transfers of their customer's funds from savings to checking accounts. This was a practice in the 1920s, to which we may now be about to revert, although Congress and the savings and loan industry may seek to block such transfers. If we cannot make *de jure* what is now *de facto* but inefficient, then regulation may, by an end run, allow banks to pass on to depositors profits in excess of marginal costs. Forty-odd years after the prohibition of interest payments on demand deposits, the time may be ripe to undo that mistake.

With respect to ceilings on time deposits, as Homer notes, these have introduced cyclical disturbances into financial intermediary markets, yet the prospects for removing the constraints on interest rates paid on these deposits and expanding the availability of deposit funds appear dim. Consumers would clearly be gainers if the ceilings were phased out. However, commercial banks are worried about potential short-term costs. Thrift institutions, that have been promised, as a *quid pro quo*, entry into product markets formerly limited to commercial banks, nevertheless, are concerned about the loss of what seems to them the protection of Regulation Q. As Homer notes, the supervisory agencies have generally favored the status quo. Thus, too many special interests are unwilling to risk dismantling a system they have come to live with, fearful of the costs of adaptation to a new and clearly more efficient system. This legacy of the New Deal is an incubus, the term Homer rightly uses.

Restrictions on Multi-Function Banking

Homer discusses bank supervision and refers to the desirability of reducing the regulation of commercial banks. The banking industry is certainly a highly regulated one, since regulations govern entry and exit, portfolio composition, firm structure, and prices. I would like to focus my comments on the New Deal effort to restrict commercial banking to what was regarded as its traditional field —short-term self-liquidating commercial loans—and to condemn operations in the field of capital financing and real estate loans.

The basis for this view was the *real bills doctrine* of bank examiners that governed their evaluation of banks in the 1920s and 1930s. The alleged weaknesses of the banking system because of the extension of the activities of banks beyond the traditional field do not explain the bank failures of 1929-1933. Had the Federal Reserve prevented the decline in the quantity of money and lent freely to sound banks, the massive bank failure rate would not have occurred. The trend toward formation of groups of banks offering a full range of financial services that had begun in the 1920s was interrupted by the New Deal misreading of what went wrong in 1929-1933. Innovations in banking operations and the search for more efficient ways of financial intermediation by commercial banks were retarded for the next 3 decades. The dramatic increase in the use of the one-bank holding company since the late 1950s takes up the thread of innovative banking that the New Deal broke. Initiative, having been stifled for some 3 decades by the trauma of the depression and the mass of regulation, has reasserted itself.

CHANGES WITH RESPECT TO THE FEDERAL RESERVE SYSTEM

Consolidation of Power within the Reserve System

Homer regards the elimination of the Secretary of the Treasury and the Comptroller from membership on the Board of Governors by the Banking Act of 1935 as being only cosmetic and of no great significance. I wonder whether the presence of the Secretary of the Treasury on the Board during the war and postwar pegging of yields on government securities by the Federal Reserve might not have permanently subverted the Federal Reserve to the British style of subservience to Treasury demands.

Homer refers to the Open Market Investment Committee of five members which operated from 1922 through 1929 as being superior in its functioning to the present FOMC. This I interpret as an expression of regret that the center of power within the system shifted from New York, the dominant member of the Open Market Investment Committee, to Washington. With the death of Benjamin Strong, the Committee lost its leadership role in the system. Had Strong lived, the structural change in the administration of open market operations, first to the twelve Reserve Bank governors, and then to the Board of Governors with five Bank representatives would probably not have occurred. In the half-century since Strong's death, no figure of comparable vision and comprehension of the system's potentialities has come to the fore.

Homer notes that the record of monetary growth was more stable from 1945 to 1967 than from 1918 to 1940. The record for the past 10 years has been less reassuring, and the Board of Governors has come increasingly under the surveillance of the Congress. There is no indication yet that Congressional overview has improved the record.

Power to Alter Reserve Requirements

Homer discusses the disastrous use the Board of Governors made in 1936-1938 of the power it acquired in the Banking Act of 1935 to double reserve requirements. In other contexts, he has referred to developments that complicate the measurement of the money supply. In my opinion, the most damaging aspect of the power to alter reserve requirements since the 1936-1938 episode is the multiplication of reserve categories for deposits that the Board has introduced. The splintering of reserve requirements has made it more difficult for the Federal Reserve to predict the results of any policy action.

Broadened Powers to Regulate Credit

The power to regulate credit conferred on the Federal Reserve in the Roosevelt era was based, as Homer notes, on the belief that credit during the 1920s had been unsound and had contributed to the economic collapse. It reflected a judgment that the banking problems of the early 1930s derived in considerable measure from the stock market boom and the participation of banks in the boom as direct lenders and as agents for others. The Banking Act of 1933 endorsed this judgment, subjecting member banks to severe reprisal for undue use of bank credit

> for the speculative carrying of or trading in securities, real estate, or commodities, or for any other purpose inconsistent with the maintenance of sound credit conditions.

Consumer credit was likewise condemned. The Securities Exchange Act granted the System power to impose margin requirements on security loans. All of the controls introduced in the years since the Roosevelt era reflect the belief that the market allocates credit improperly. The interventionist philosophy has been blind to the fact that controls have simply led to the rerouting of the sources of funds.

Even more serious is the fact that the regulation of credit distracts the Federal Reserve from its main responsibility—regulating the supply of money.

SUMMARY

My assessment of the New Deal banking reforms is that they were based on a misinterpretation of developments in the 1920s and of the banking collapse of 1929-1933. The one reform that I regard as a contribution to economic stability was the establishment of deposit insurance. The regulation of interest on bank deposits was a mistake from which we have not yet extricated the economy. The restriction of multi-function banking retarded commercial bank innovation for

3 decades. The power to alter reserve requirements has been one of the ways in which the Federal Reserve has complicated monetary control, while the exercise of power to control specific uses of credit has been futile. The Federal Reserve has grown in regulatory responsibilities with no indication that these have promoted the discharge of its main responsibility, that of managing wisely the growth of the money supply.

REFERENCES

Burns, A. F. *Vital issues of banking legislation*. Address at the 83rd Annual Convention of the Kentucky Bankers Association, Louisville, Kentucky. Federal Reserve release, Sept. 12, 1977.

Chapter 6

On Understanding the Birth and Evolution of the Securities and Exchange Commission: Where Are We in the Theory of Regulation?

ROBERT J. MACKAY and JOSEPH D. REID, JR.

INTRODUCTION

The Securities and Exchange Commission (SEC) is unique. To be sure, it was created by the New Deal at a time when many other regulatory agencies were being established, but there the resemblance stops. The SEC is set apart, first, by its restrained growth rate. The expenditures of the SEC, since its beginning, have grown at only three-fifths the rate of expenditure growth of other federal agencies.[1] Second, the SEC has grown less rapidly than the industry it regulates (Stig-

---

[1] Stigler (1972b) calculates the annual growth of SEC expenditure from 1934 to 1969 at 4.6% and of expenditure by the other major independent federal regulatory agencies at 7.8%. SEC employment figures from selected *Securities and Exchange Commission Annual Reports*; federal civil service employment from *Historical Statistics* (Bureau of the Census, 1975, Series Y-311, p. 1102). Further evidence of SEC singularity is that its expenditures were constant through 1955 (*SEC Annual Reports*), while expenditures of the other federal regulatory agencies annually increased 7% (Stigler, 1972b). As Benston points out in his discussion, SEC budget and employment growth rates are now approaching total federal growth rates.

To be sure, neither employees nor budget unambiguously measure the size or impact

ler, 1972b, p. 153). Third, and most important, the SEC recently agreed with efforts to *reduce* its regulation of securities markets: Between 1968 and 1975, the SEC effected a change in the New York Stock Exchange (NYSE) from fixed to negotiated commissions.

Few of the many theories of regulation accommodate change toward more competition, and fewer yet accommodate a change so rapid as that which SEC has accomplished. When a regulatory agency changes from the encouragement of cartelization to the encouragement of competition within a major part of its domain, there is cause for investigation. The SEC, in spite of its unique development, resembles other regulatory agencies in its establishment and general goals. These qualities of uniqueness from and similarity to the other regulatory agencies give merit to a close study of the SEC.

To begin such study, we first survey existing theories of regulation and the political processes implicit in each of these theories along with the insights they provide about the birth and evolution of regulatory agencies. We relate these theories to the establishment of the SEC and to empirical studies of the effects of SEC regulation in order to determine the gaps in our understanding of the SEC as well as the shortcomings of the contending theories. We conclude that existing theories of regulation are incomplete, but admit that we may be damning the theories for the inadequacies of prior empirical work. To supplement previous models of regulation, we emphasize the roles of crisis and of discretionary power, then we substantiate their importance to understanding the history of the SEC. The theories are also applied to the more recent history of the SEC, the period of pro-competitive reform since 1968, to determine how well we understand the forces leading to regulatory reform. In short, we use the history of the SEC to raise questions about the profession's current understanding of the process of regulation.

THEORIES OF ECONOMIC REGULATION

Theories of economic regulation abound and are surveyed by Jordan (1972), Posner (1974), Peltzman (1976), and Reid (1977). The main theories are: (*a*) the

---

of an agency. The IRS, for example, is small in size and budget, yet it affects the economy mightily. "Off-budget" expenditures of SEC include the salaries of the many financial accountants and securities lawyers who collect the numbers and fill out the forms required by SEC and the bills of the printers who print the public reports stimulated by the SEC, *ad nauseam*. A related measure of the off-budget impact of SEC comes from the libraries of Southern Methodist University. The law library catalogues 100 separate publications under SEC (histories, laws, studies, reports on securities markets, issues of *Securities Law Review*, and the like) that fill 26 feet of shelf space; the government documents library adds 125 feet of shelf space, although some duplicate law library holdings. On-budget or off-budget impact is, we argue in succeeding text, a strategic decision. In the past, off-budget expenditures quickly gained economic impact and political independence for an agency.

"public interest" or "market failure" theory that regulation is a correction for the failure of private markets, (b) the "capture" theory that regulation is the result of a special interest's capture of government's power to coerce, (c) the "many interests" theory that many special interest groups share direction of the government's power to coerce, and (d) the "public choice" approach that stresses various aspects of the dynamics of regulation and is perhaps best summarized by the phrase "politicians and bureaucrats matter."

The public interest or market failure theory holds that government intervention into market processes is a means through which individuals join together in collective political action to correct inefficiencies and inequities that result from market failures. Although the theory of market failure has led predominantly to normative theories of government intervention, it also has positive, predictive content.[2] For example, to value a security requires analysis of complex information (Ripley, 1926). No private investor will bear the total burden of obtaining an optimal amount of information and of performing an optimal analysis because no investor buys all of the issue. Thus no investor captures all the benefits of an optimal evaluation of the worth of a security, and as no investor buys continuously, the private cost of the training prerequisite to accurate valuation of securities' issues is too high. Thus, the dispersal of benefits among the public leads to scant and unskillful evaluation of securities by investors. Because everyone gains from the correction of market failures due to externalities, public goods, natural monopoly, destructive competition, or fraud, the public interest theory predicts the emergence of broad based citizen demands for government intervention or regulation to achieve these ends. If, moreover, the political process is responsive to these demands, this theory implies that government intervention will result from the experience of market failure.

Many others, however, argue that the costs of participation in democratic politics and the imperfection of political information make government regulation in the public interest unlikely.[3] This is true because the public interest is so broadly based and the individual gain from each achievement of the public interest is so small (although the collective sum is large) that no one demands that the public interest be served. Rather, each wants his special interest served. Accordingly, this special interest school predicts that government will serve narrow private interests.

In fact, there is evidence that the public interest is not the guide of government intervention. "Some 15 years of theoretical and empirical research . . . have demonstrated that regulation is not positively correlated with the presence of external economies or diseconomies or with monopolistic market structure" (Pos-

---

[2] See Buchanan and Tullock (1962) for a detailed elaboration of this view of government activity.

[3] See Aranson and Ordeshook (1976), Auster (1974), Goldin (1975), Stigler (1971), and Tullock (1971) for examples.

ner, 1974, p. 336). However, it is not obvious which, if any, interest is served in each instance of government regulation.

Some scholars argue that regulation is pure producer protection with the government acting as a perfect, profit maximizing broker for a private cartel.[4] Government intervention, in this view, attains or preserves some industrialists' interest at the expense of other industrialists and the public (Jordan, 1972; Kolko, 1965). Others still hold that "as a rule, regulation is acquired by the industry and designed and operated primarily for its benefit" (Stigler, 1971, p. 3).

In contrast, Buchanan and Tideman (1974) hypothesize that government switches from protection of producers to protection of consumers when a market crisis wrecks the customary balance between producer interest and voter apathy. In response to a large and sudden rise in a relative price, for example, the government becomes a broker for a consumers' buying monopsony, rather than continuing as a broker for a producers' selling monopoly. Thereby, government restores past equity. Hughes (1977) documents the breadth and variety of government interventions in the economy. He, too, finds market crises to be the source of government intervention. Hughes (1977, pp. 7-8) does not agree, however, that the government invariably cartelizes consumers or producers and he accepts the theory that today's political outcomes are nothing more than the random residue of 200 years of past efforts to disperse the shocks felt by the economy.

To integrate economic logic with political history, Peltzman (1976) argues that politician-regulators efficiently transform consumer and producer surpluses of unregulated goods markets into political income. This is accomplished by redistributing these surpluses, through regulation and taxation, among contending political interest groups so that the politician's marginal gains and losses are just balanced. The variety and evolution of political outcomes are attributed to changes in marginal political benefits. These, in turn, are induced by exogenous changes in the political effectiveness of different interest groups or by changes in the determinants of the size of the goods market surpluses to be redistributed. The end result: many outcomes in accord with many interests.[5]

These attempts to understand regulation are a significant advance over the original public interest theory of automatic and beneficial economic regulation for they build on the idea that economic regulation and other public goods are demanded by constituents and supplied by politicans in a political market, just as widgets, lollipops, and a myriad of other goods are demanded by consumers and supplied by producers in the goods market. These market models of govern-

[4] Posner (1972b, 1974), however, documents the variety of political outcomes at odds with the special interest hypothesis.

[5] For like models of regulator-politicians balancing the marginal gains and losses of special interests, see Brock and Magee (1975) and Goodman (1977).

ment, however, make the political market resemble the goods market too closely, that is, the politician orders up and the regulator-bureaucrat faithfully supplies what the political market most wants, just as the store owner orders up and the clerk faithfully supplies what the shoppers want in a competitive goods market. On the one hand, politicians are seen to be constrained by fierce political competition to respond to the demands of effective interest groups. On the other hand, the administrative agency and its employees, the regulators, are seen to be passive servants of the legislature who attempt to enforce and carry out political bargains struck between the legislature and politically effective interest groups (Posner, 1972b). Thus, politicians and their perfect agents, regulators, slavishly serve and do not change political demand. The supply of outcomes is independent of demand, and equilibrium in the political market, just as in the private goods market, is unique.

In sum, it is only the addition of votes to dollars as the means of announcing wants that differentiates the political market from the goods market in the analyses of regulation considered above. Although it must be admitted that the uniqueness of political outcomes is temporal, that admission does not influence these analyses. Indeed, Stigler (1972a) even equates the variety of *potential* outcomes of a political issue—a Democrat or a Republican may be elected, Braniff or Pan American may be awarded the London–Dallas route—with the variety of actual outcomes in the goods market. Peltzman (1976) goes further: He argues that the actual political outcome is so diverse (the politician-regulator operates at the margin to reduce opposition) that there is no significant analytical difference between the goods market and the political market. Finally, only the source of their paychecks differentiates civil servant bureaucrats from captains or clerks of industry: All serve faithfully, if perhaps indirectly, the (appropriately aggregated) public.

In truth, the political market differs greatly from the goods market. Outcomes are coercive in the political market.[6] Furthermore, there is a scant assurance that the supply of political outcomes will respond to shifts in demand. At the least, there does not exist the same degree of certainty that a political market outcome will change as certainly as will a goods market outcome in light of new conditions. On the one hand, changed conditions might not be sufficiently general or noteworthy for political recognition and response. On the other hand, even if there is response, it will not necessarily bring relief; political bargains, once reopened, can resettle further from, as well as closer to, the social optimum.

One reason for such perversities is the one that prompted dissatisfactions with

---

[6] This and the several paragraphs following draw heavily on Reid (1977, pp. 307–311). Similar dissatisfactions with existing models of political activity are expressed by Hirshleifer (1976), Posner (1974) and Weaver (1977).

the public interest theory of regulation: Consumers of political outcomes articulate their changed conditions and their new desires with an effectiveness that varies with their intensity of interest and their ease in delivering political currency—some function of votes and income (Davis and North, 1971; Olson, 1965; Stigler, 1972b). Such considerations are doubly important for independent regulatory agencies because a group's voting strength is filtered through several steps —houses of Congress to committees to subcommittees to agency, in a textbook case of delegated democracy—and cash payments are illegal.

A related reason for the lack of response to changed political conditions is that initial political decisions redistribute wealth and therewith create or strengthen a constituency of support for the status quo. At a minimum, such support for an existing political decision is proportional to the cost of abandoning the existing wealth for that of an unestablished source. Most likely, normal risk aversion will increase support for the status quo over support for a new situation in that the current wealth will seem more secure than its possible replacement.

However, the most important reason for perversities in political response is that politicians and regulators want to maximize their welfare. The attenuation of reaction to their decisions, induced by the filtering and bunchiness of votes, lets them increase their utility directly through the content of their decisions, as well as indirectly through the effects of their decisions upon their salary and tenure. The entrenched politician or regulator will as often balance *his* marginal interests as those of the public.[7] Thus, recent alternatives to special interest and many interests theories of government regulation start with the discretionary power of politicians and regulators, so that politicians and bureaucrats do indeed matter.

The politicians and bureaucrats matter school emphasizes that politicians and regulators are imperfect agents at the birth as well as throughout the life of an administrative agency.[8] That is, of course, the corollary of discretionary power. However, if bureaucrats do not selflessly serve politicans and if politicians do not selflessly serve some public, what do they do? Niskanen (1971, 1975) suggests that a top bureaucrat strives to maximize the size of his bureau. That is too simple, however. Eckert (1973) shows that a bureaucrat's maximand is influenced by his future interest: A bureaucrat expecting to leave the government soon is less interested in the size or rate of growth of his bureau, for instance,

---

[7] The politician-regulator who is not yet entrenched will, of course, pay more attention to the public's marginal interests—distorted as they are by the political transmission process. However, from first appointment or election, the politician-regulator has significantly cheaper opportunities for direct utility maximization, and he will use them.

[8] See Barro (1972) and Wagner (1975) for models dealing explicitly with the control of politicians and bureaucrats. Ehrlich and Posner (1974) develop a model of administrative failure resulting from multiplying demands in the legislature.

than in the "quiet life" or the marketability of his "human capital." Kau and Rubin (1978) verify the theory that legislators seek more ideological purity than seems consistent with maximization of votes or spoils.[9] Clearly, politicians are not mere brokers who represent or adjudicate among factors.

Once politicians and regulators are no longer viewed as passive servants of either public or special interests, it is but a small step further to suggest that politicians and regulators flock to politics rather than to industry because they *want* discretionary power.[10] Discretion for what? To remedy society's wrongs (likely made apparent by "some academic scribbler of a few years back" [Keynes, 1936, p. 383])? To gain the quiet life? To build up human capital for future use? Or to exchange current power for immediate cash in the marketplace? Tastes vary.

We can, however, predict the evolution of a regulatory agency from vigor to lethargy and from partnership with Congress and the president to independence from both. Because discretionary power is costly to acquire in the goods market, the supply of would-be holders of discretionary power who are available to the government is highly elastic at a low expected wage. The halls of Congress are crammed with would-be regulators who compete by claiming the special talents to mitigate this or that problem. Who, then, will generate or await the call of crisis to found an agency? The zealot, of course, who subsidizes his long hours in queue with the psychic income of anticipated salvation and recognition. Furthermore, the zealot's devotion to a problem prepares him for putting together its remedy and for drawing its accompanying organization chart. When *his* crisis beckons, if ever, he is ready. The alternate regulator, in search of a quiet life, seeks *any* berth, and, therefore, does not prepare so completely for one particular berth. Accordingly, founders of regulatory agencies more likely will be vigorous zealots. Their successors, more likely, will seek more private and therefore less visible rewards. They will seem lethargic and inefficient, for the preservation and enlargement of their discretion will be more important to the successors than will the accomplishment of some coercive public reform. Hence, the successors, more likely, will seek independence from Congress and the president by establishing and sustaining a powerful constituency outside government or by innocuous inaction. Unfortunately, to cloud the contrast between zealots and their successors, zealots who suspect their call to be unsupported will also strive

---

[9] Faithfulness to an ideology, to be sure, is an efficient response by politicians to the high cost of becoming known by voters (Reid, 1977).

[10] A step consistent with the facts, as well. *The Wall Street Journal* recently interviewed retiring Congressmen to find out why a record number was retiring just after "voting reform" legislation had further raised the incumbents' election advantage. A principal reason was that constituents now wanted too much immediate and particular service from Congressmen. Although voting reforms made reelection even more probable, the Congressmen's reduced discretionary power made retirement even more desirable.

for an independent power base. Thus, purposive and predictable exploitation of political institutions by regulators explains the creation and later transformations of regulatory agencies.[11]

While all the above theories of regulation find some support in facts, we think that the last or "politicians and bureaucrats matter" approach seems most meaningful, even though it is least developed. The following brief history of the SEC examines the relevance of the various theories of economic regulation and, we believe, supports our conclusion.

THE BIRTH OF SEC AND THE EXPLANATORY POWER OF ALTERNATIVE THEORIES OF REGULATION

The Securities Act of 1933 and the Securities and Exchange Act of 1934 that established the SEC had two major stated purposes: (1) protection of investors, and (2) promotion of the public interest as this interest is affected by trading in securities. Together, the acts were to prevent the prices of stocks and bonds from going any direction but up. These goals were to be achieved "by policies designed: (*a*) to require full disclosure of material facts on securities sold in the primary and secondary markets, (*b*) to prevent manipulation of securities' prices, (*c*) to curb unfair trading practices, (*d*) to maintain orderly and liquid markets, and (*e*) to control 'excessive' use of credit" (Friend, 1976, p. 1).

Most experts agree that the acts were in the public interest. Historians of the New Deal, for example, agree that the Crash of 1929 resulted from manipulations and frauds practiced on an investing public that was kept in the dark about the "true" worth of the securities they held (de Bedts, 1964; Galbraith, 1955; Parrish, 1970; Ripley, 1926). More to the point, historians agree that common stock investors saw themselves as victims of frauds and manipulations in 1929, so that the acts were in some sense at public request, as well as in the public interest.

Legislation to guarantee profits to investors or, at the least, to prevent financiers from fleecing the lambs in the hinterlands was not new to America in 1933. Many states, especially those with a "progressive" heritage, regulated sales of securities by 1920 (Loss, 1961, Chap. 1; Parrish, 1970, Chap. 1). As did federal regulation, the typical state law required the disclosure of the issuer's assets and

---

[11] Our explanation of the typical life cycle is very different from that of Posner (1974, pp. 339-340). We suggest that purposive exploitation of political institutions by bureaucrats, rather than the shifted attention of legislator-monitors, explains why agency performance declines as legislative oversight declines. Effective oversight is not continuous and is not reestablished, we argue, because the agency uses its first freedom to gain independence from the legislature by creating another constituency. This is also the theme of Weaver's (1977, Chap.1) examination of the birth and evolution of the social security system in the United States.

liabilities, the control of selling expenses, and the licensing of sellers. State laws could claim parentage in England's Companies Act of 1844 and later. In preparation for the Companies Act of 1900, for instance, the Lord Davey Committee (Loss, 1961) reported:

> ... it must be generally acknowledged that a person who is invited to subscribe to a new undertaking has practically no opportunity of making any independent inquiry before coming to a decision...
> It is therefore of the highest importance that the prospectus upon which the public are invited to subscribe shall not only not contain any misrepresentation but shall satisfy a high standard of good faith (p. 6).

In sum, long prior to 1933, securities were known to be prone to fraud, and the needed offset was in advance disclosure of the company's worth and of the credentials of securities salesmen.[12]

New facts and new theories, however, suggested that state regulation of securities was inadequate. The 1920s yielded international swindles and culminated in the Crash. Fear of fraud was then so great that it seemed Americans would not again invest. New theories implied that rules beyond mere corporate disclosure were needed to restore investors' confidence. Berle and Means (1932), for instance, contended that corporate managements could thwart investors' interests at will. Disclosing the fact that management could despoil bond and shareholders was inadequate remedy, for management insulated itself from stockholders' oversight and from bond covenants by use of irrational corporate structures and interlocking directorates. What was required, therefore, was rationalization of corporate structures, public oversight of managers and directors to stop abuses of the discretionary power that remained, control of stock exchanges to stop manipulations of old issues, and more and better disclosure. Surely the public interest demanded that Congress pass the "truth in securities" laws.

On the surface, then, *the birth* of the SEC would appear to be adequately explained by the public interest or market failure theory. It does not necessarily denigrate the SEC's devotion to the public interest to observe that most of its regulations in theory are unneeded and, in fact, are unable to improve the securities market. For example, the theory of a competitive securities market with timely justice or perfect remembrance of fraud implies that all information rele-

---

[12] In his discussion, Benston infers that the federal Securities Acts had little link to "Blue Sky" progressivism, for, unlike many states' acts, the federal acts eschewed evaluation of the worth of traded securities. Benston, likewise, questions the extent of precedent in the English Companies Acts, for the English acts called only for financial disclosure by corporations and did not regulate brokers, salesmen, and the like. We believe that regulation of securities salesmen reflects the progressive heritage and that eschewment of valuation reflects the pragmatic heritage of the New Deal. But we agree that *post hoc, ergo propter hoc* may direct our judgement. De Bedts (1970, ch. 1), Loss (1961, ch. 1), McCormick (1948, ch. 1), and Parrish (1970, ch. 1) agree with us.

vant for securities holders would be published and published by its least cost supplier—usually, but not always, the firm. In this theory, some firms would disclose sales—where sales indicated profits—others, cash flow; others, assets and forecasts, and so on, just as firms did prior to SEC (Benston, 1973).[13] Uniform and conservative (no forecasts or judgements) accounting, as required by the SEC, would make disallowed but wanted information costly to obtain and would make firms incur the costs of producing irrelevant information. If securities markets previously were efficient, then required disclosure would reduce corporate earnings and increase their perceived uncertainty, and so would lower, rather than raise, the prices of claims to those earnings. In fact, evidence suggests that required disclosure did not raise the prices of old securities (Benston, 1969a, 1969b, 1973). If registration requirements did improve performance of new issues on regulated exchanges, it seems that they did so by driving lesser known issues into private placements, that is, by raising the costs of capital to smaller companies (Benston, 1969a, 1969b; Stone, 1973).

SEC rules prohibiting such stock market actions as *wash sales, matched orders,* and like manipulations, are also unneeded if the public interest theory is relevant, because exchanges have an interest in stopping such activities. SEC rules restricting insider trading may be defensible on equity grounds, but there is evidence that these rules were largely unenforced from 1934 to 1961. Moreover, increased enforcement efforts after 1961 led to little, if any, effects on the volume or profitability of insider trading (Jaffe, 1974, p. 119). It is not possible, at this time, to say whether or not SEC regulation reduced the extent of attempted manipulation.[14] Casual evidence (Pecora, 1939, for example) on the extent of attempted manipulation is of only slight interest since intent and actual outcome may differ greatly. Finally, SEC regulation of "speculative practices," from limits on use of *puts and calls* to constraints on (and now proposed abolition of) floor traders, reduces the efficiency of the securities market.

In short, those empirical studies that measure the benefits of SEC regulation offer little support for the public interest or market failure theory of regulation. Still some might argue that the failure to find broad based benefits results from the lack of refined testing. Alternatively, one need not insist on a correspondence between intended and actual beneficiaries or between perceptions and reality, and, therefore, may dismiss the lack of actual benefits as irrelevant. The rules controlling speculative activities, manipulation, and insider trading had broad public support at the time of enactment, regardless of current theories and tests. Many thought that the required disclosure would benefit honest issuers, as well as buyers of securities. Some still think that disclosure is beneficial (Sommer, 1974). However, before accepting this ad hoc defense of the public interest

---

[13] For a more detailed discussion of these points, see Gonedes (1975).
[14] Mackay, currently, is examining the behavior of the prices of various stocks that, allegedly, were the subject of manipulation by pool operations in the pre-SEC period.

TABLE 6.1
Major NYSE Commission Rate Changes Since 1926[a]

Date	Description of rate schedule
1/1/26	Fixed charge per share. The level of the per share charge increased with the price per share, but at a decreasing rate of increase.
1/3/38	All commission rates increased by 11%.
3/16/42	All commission rates increased by 10%.
11/3/47	New sliding scale of commissions based upon the value of a round lot of 100 shares. Average increase of 20%.
9/1/53	Average increase of about 18%.
5/1/58	Average increase of 13%.
12/5/68	Volume discount on trades of more than 1,000 shares. Average decrease of about 7%.
4/2/71	Small trade surcharge of $15 per trade of less than 1,000 shares.
4/5/71	Negotiated commission rates for orders over $500,000 ordered by SEC.
4/31/72	Negotiated commission rates for orders over $300,000 ordered by SEC. Small trade surcharge ends.
5/1/75	Negotiated commission rates on all orders.

[a]Source: Schwert (1977a, p. 144).

foundation for the SEC, it seems wise to consider first the other theories of regulation.

If the SEC has not served the public interest, what interest or many special interests has it served? An obvious special interest is the brokerage industry. Two hypotheses must be examined. First, was SEC regulation acquired by the brokerage industry? Second, if not, was the SEC then captured, at some later date, by the brokerage industry?

There is evidence that members of stock exchanges did not want any regulation. If regulation were inevitable, however, they argued for flexible and separate regulation. "Flexible" meant regulation by commission, rather than by statute, and "separate" meant regulation by a new commission; the SEC, rather than by the Federal Trade Commission or some other existing commission. Spokesmen for the New York Stock Exchange (NYSE) and the regional stock exchanges stressed the need for fast rectification of bad provisions and emphasized the separate interests of the smaller exchanges.

Although initially opposed to regulation, the brokerage industry and the NYSE, in particular, may have captured SEC. The price fixing powers of the NYSE, one of America's oldest cartels, were not seriously challenged by the SEC until the late 1960s, for example (Baxter, 1970; Doede, 1967). In fact, from the passage of the Securities and Exchange Act of 1934 that exempted national exchanges from antitrust legislation until 1968, the NYSE effected five increases in the minimum rate schedule without serious objection from the SEC (see Table 6.1).

Schwert (1977a), however, concludes that the formation of SEC hurt members of NYSE and AMEX financially. To reach his conclusion, Schwert (1977a, 1977b) notes that the prices of stock exchange seats capitalize expected monopoly rents from exchange membership. He relates expected rents to volume and to expected share prices (that determine per share commissions).[15] Schwert (1977a, p. 140) calculates that the proposed regulation halved the prices of NYSE and AMEX seats and that no later "capture" of SEC recouped these losses for exchange members.

Schwert's (1977a) analysis is ingenious and suggestive. It is inconclusive, however. Most important, more than changed expectations of share prices and volumes would affect the price of exchange seats. Investors' demand for a risk premium, for example, would raise the rate of discount and thereby depress the price of stock exchange seats. There are, in fact, many reasons to suspect that investors' general confidence, and, therefore, rate of discount, changed widely in the early 1930s. At the same time that the forerunner of the Securities Act of 1934 was introduced into Congress, newspapers reported investors' fears about the abandonment of the gold standard. Newspapers also emblazoned the government's abrupt cancellation of all private airmail contracts.[16] Prices of stocks, as well as of exchange seats, tumbled again when Roosevelt demanded "a stock exchange regulation bill with teeth in it" in a March 27, 1934, address to Congress.[17] Plausibly, fear for the future of all investments, including the future of stock exchange seats, increased in February-March, 1934, the period singled out by Schwert (1977a) to measure the impact of the SEC.

Schwert (1977a) does not contradict our interpretation that general fear for the future lowered the price of all investments. Indeed, Schwert (1977a, pp. 142 and 144) finds no adverse SEC effect on trading volumes or commissions prior to 1968. Neither does he find monthly upward revisions of seat prices to be in response to the significant weakening of the bill between its February introduction and June enactment (Schwert, 1977a, pp. 140-142).[18] This may reflect the

---

[15] Accordingly, Schwert (1977a, p. 134-40) regresses monthly rates of NYSE and AMEX seat price changes against univariate ARIMA forecasts of rates of share prices and share volume changes. He relates residuals from these regressions to the proposal for and subsequent federal regulation of stock exchanges.

[16] See the *New York Times*, February 5, 1934, p. 25; February 10, p. 21; and February 11; pp. 7 and 11, section W, for representative stories.

[17] Reported in the *Wall Street Journal*, March 28, 1934, p. 17.

[18] In a front page *Wall Street Journal* (June 2, 1934), headlined "Hopeful on New Stock Act," NYSE president Richard Whitney points out that the bill passed differed significantly from the bill proposed in February (see also Parrish, 1970, p. 118.) In particular, the Securities Exchange Act, of 1934, did *not*: entrust regulation to the FTC; segregate brokers from dealers; outlaw *puts, calls, straddles,* and other options; or abolish *odd lot traders* or *specialists*.

6. Where Are We in the Theory of Regulation? 113

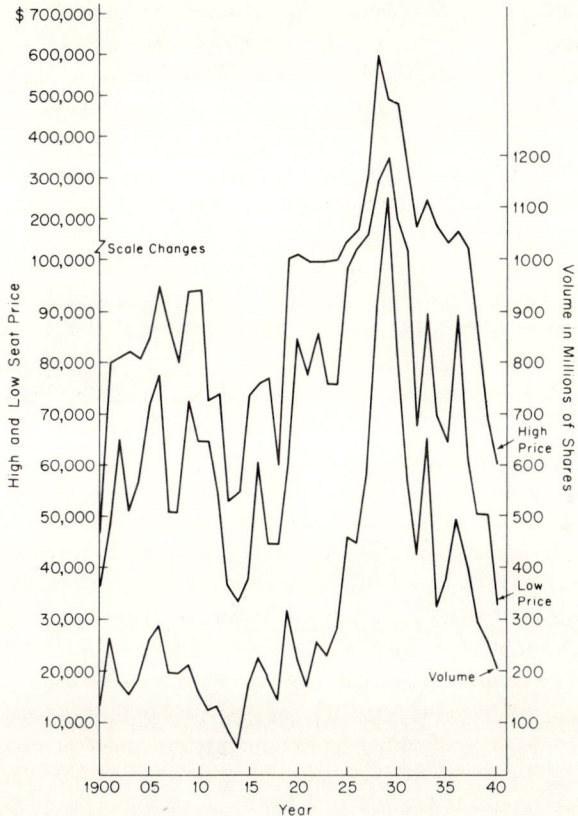

Figure 6.1. Seat prices and share volume: 1900–1940 (from an unpublished report, Directorate of Economic and Policy Research, Securities and Exchange Commission, June, 1977).

inability of his model to measure solely the impact of the SEC on brokers' anticipated profits in this hectic period.[19] Some evidence of heightened uncertainty is revealed in Figure 6.1, that graphs high and low seat prices and annual volume for the NYSE. Before 1926, the respective ratios of high and low price to volume were about .00044 and .00032, and annual low prices usually exceeded two-thirds of annual highs. In 1931, however, the ratio of low seat price to volume went to about .00018. Annual high prices, in contrast, fell more slowly and erratically. Divided by volume of the same or of the succeeding year (to allow

---

[19] One measure of the confusion of this period is the 20%+ increase in standard deviation of the residuals from comparable seat price equations for 1930–1937 and for 1926–1945 (Schwert, 1977a, table 5, p. 140), even when the March, 1934, dummy variable is employed.

for the declining trend of volume), this ratio resisted decline from the halcyon levels of 1927-1929 and did not get back to its customary three-to-two relation with the low price-volume ratio until 1936.[20] Thus, tumbling stock prices, accelerating direct federal intervention in many parts of the economy, and erratic and protracted changes in seat prices suggest that general fear for the future, rather than anticipation of a specific burden from watered-down and ineffectual regulation, lowered the price of stock exchange seats in the 1930s.

The existing empirical evidence that is relevant to understanding the birth of the SEC causes a perplexing situation. On the one hand, the studies by Stigler (1964), Benston (1969b, 1973, 1976), Stone (1973), and Jaffe (1974) show little evidence of broadly based benefits resulting from SEC regulation and, thereby, cast doubt on the market failure theory. On the other hand, the study by Schwert (1977a), in spite of its shortcomings, casts doubt on the special interest or capture theory. There is no fully adequate explanation of the birth of SEC apart from the importance of market crisis in setting the stage for regulation.

Before dismissing altogether the special interest or many special interests theories, however, it will be worthwhile to look at other groups that benefit from SEC regulation. Two groups deserve special attention: certified public accountants and securities lawyers.

Well before the Crash of 1929 or the Senate hearings of 1933-1934, accountants had been pushing for financial disclosure. The panic of 1907 prompted an editorial in *The Journal of Accountancy*. It attributed the panic to sudden public distrust of corporate management and, in order to restore trust, recommended that independent certified public accountants examine the books of all corporations (Carey, 1969, pp. 54-55). The speciality of accountants' interest was revealed sharply in their response to the Corporation Excise Tax Law of 1909. That law proposed to tax corporations on net *cash* income, cash receipts less cash expenses and cash losses. Such a law obviously provided little stimulus to the demand for accountants. Accordingly, major accounting firms lobbied instead for an excise tax on "profits," that they proposed to calculate as "true" income less expenses incurred, losses ascertained, interest accrued, and with an allowance for depreciation. While the accountants' efforts proved fruitless in Congress, they were more fruitful with the law's administrator: the Secretary of the Treasury permitted the use of and firms took advantage of other-than-cash accounting methods which reduced taxes (Carey, 1969, pp. 64-77). Recalling this and other then-recent legislation, the incoming president of the American

---

[20] To be sure, Figure 6.1 is in levels, and these patterns only directly observed, not revealed by a precise analysis of precise data. At best, they are suggestive. However, they agree with other, common observations of the unsettled expectations of investors in the 1930s. They do not defy common sense, as does Schwert's (1977a, pp. 140-142) interpretation that mere introduction of a bill immediately and permanently lowered exchange seats' prices, although the legislation was substantially modified before its enactment and did not affect the hypothesized determinants of seat prices, share prices, or trading volume.

Association of Public Accountants observed that "foolish laws and more foolish laws, relating to taxation and regulation, will not diminish the income of the professional accountant" (Carey, 1969, p. 72). He did not, however, urge that accountants encourage foolish laws. Rather, he urged that accountants support federal control (Carey, 1969):

> The people are not afraid of big business. They want it, but they know that it must be controlled.... Without a knowledge of profits, there can be no regulation, no control.... Therefore, every plan of federal control must provide for the certification of profits and balance sheets by independent accountants (p. 73).

The American Institute of Public Accountants listened and proceeded apace to reduce the supply of accountants by upgrading professional ethics and standards and to increase demand through cooperation with politicians and regulators in the drafting of new laws. Thus, "respected citizen[s] . . . [of] unimpeachable integrity . . . [with] access to influential members of Congress and of the executive branch" were hired to lobby (Carey, 1969, p. 183). The value of such lobbyists in advancing accountants' special interests was high: the preceding quote by John Carey, longtime editor of *The Journal of Accountancy,* describes paid lobbyist Judge J. Henry Covington who helped Congress draft the Securities Act of 1933. Judge Covington led the bill's evolution from its early form in which it had only one reference to independent audits to the final act which required independent audits of all registration statements. Indeed, Carey (1969, p. 202) points out that the requirement of disclosure in accordance with generally accepted accounting practices put certified public accountants on their feet.

The growth of the securities bar is not so well documented. Quantifications are somewhat indirect and ambiguous. However, the card catalog entries and library shelf span occupied by securities legislation[1] do provide copious evidence. There is little doubt about the nurture of the securities bar by SEC and securities legislation.

In summary, the history of SEC development leads to the conclusions (*a*) that the typical regulatory agency attempts to serve many interests (the public interest, this and that special interest, the bureaucrat's interest, and the politicians' interest), (*b*) that no interest necessarily is served well; and (*c*) that there is a set of sustainable outcomes that evolves over time and that limits actual outcomes at any time.

RECENT REGULATORY REFORM BY SEC AND THE EXPLANATORY POWER OF ALTERNATIVE THEORIES OF REGULATION

SEC failed to raise any serious objections to the five increases in the minimum commission rate schedule requested by the NYSE between 1934 and 1958.

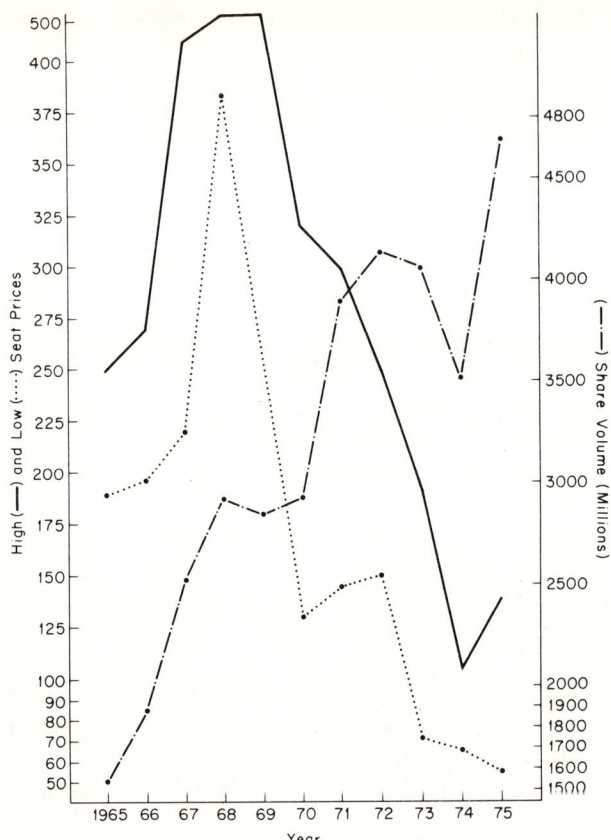

Figure 6.2. Seat prices and share volume: 1965-1975 (from an unpublished report, Directorate of Economic and Policy Research, Securities and Exchange Commission, June, 1977).

The anticompetitive characteristics of the price fixing powers of NYSE went virtually unchallenged by SEC until the late 1960s. In the spring of 1968, however, the Department of Justice, in response to a proforma request by SEC for comments on NYSE proposals to raise minimum commissions, seriously questioned the justifications for the system of minimum rates and suggested that maximum rates might be warranted. The Department of Justice brief led to a series of hearings that resulted in SEC denial of the NYSE request for changes in commission rates. In the early 1970s, the SEC continued this pro-competitive reversal of its earlier policy, requiring negotiated commission rates for orders over $500,000 in April, 1971, for orders over $300,000 in April, 1972, and for all orders in May, 1975 (see Table 6.1). These requirements sharply reduced NYSE seat prices (Schwert, 1977a, pp. 143-145), as is illustrated in Figure 6.2.

The change in a regulatory agency from encouragement of cartelization to encouragement of competition is rare. Such cartel "busting" by a regulatory agency, of course, does not detract from the public interest or market failure theory since the social gains from greater output are clear. But support for the public interest theory is certainly weakened by the existence of a 40 year lag in the SEC's response! Since this theory fails to explain the birth of the SEC and its performance up to 1968, it is unlikely to explain the recent deregulation period.

The many special interests theory (Brock & Magee, 1975; Goodman, 1977; Peltzman, 1976) can more likely explain recent reform. To test this theory, one can, first, isolate those groups that have benefited or have been hurt by a regulatory change and then look for a corresponding shift in political effectiveness that would explain the change in policy. In other words, is the change in policy quite possibly the reaction of the rational politician-regulator to changes in marginal support for or opposition to the earlier policy? The competitive environment that resulted from the unfixing of commission rates obviously benefited such customers as the large institutional investors (e.g., insurance companies, pension funds, and banks). A recent study by SEC concluded that "the average commission paid by institutions as a percent of principal decreased . . . from .84 to .51%, a decrease of 39% and for individuals from 1.73 to 1.54%, a decrease of 11% with the advent of competition (Phillips, 1978).[21] Revenue losses for broker-dealers were in line with this change in market conditions: institutional firms suffered the greatest decline, 27%, since they catered to the rate sensitive customers (Securities and Exchange Commission, 1976). Savings to investor-customers were estimated to be approximately $25 million per month for the 8 month period from May to December of 1975. This is roughly 11% of the total securities commission revenue collected (Securities and Exchange Commission, 1976).

This particular distribution of gainers (institutional investors and block traders) and losers (NYSE members) is in accord with the many special interests theory if one considers the rapid growth of institutional investors in the market since the early 1960s. From 1960 to 1970, the institutional share of trading volume on the NYSE rose by about 550%, while the share volume of individual investors rose by only 133% (Securities and Exchange Commission, 1971). More specifically, in October, 1963, the institutional share of trading volume on NYSE was 31% of public trading volume. In 1966, it had grown to 43%, and, during 1969, it reached 56%. Since then, the trend has leveled off at about 57–60% (New York Stock Exchange, 1976). The switch in SEC position can be better explained as a marginal accommodation to a new politically effective interest

---

[21] See Securities and Exchange Commission (1976) for additional details on the gains to various customer groups as well as the losses to various kinds of firms.

group, than as a sudden conversion of the SEC to the free market philosophy.[22] But the necessary catalyst was the apparently random opposition of the Department of Justice to the seventh request for an increase in commissions filed by the NYSE since the founding of SEC. The funds and other block traders then came forth in support of deregulation.

Thus, the main points to note are, first, that many interests are served. Second, it is unlikely that a regulation will be enlarged or even continued if it does not have a constituency. A constituency is *not* needed, however, to establish the first new regulation. That depends upon the enthusiasm of the regulator and the inertia of the past. Inertia can be offset with a new force, and the competitive market will produce a new force rapidly when the return is high. The rise of financial accountants and of securities lawyers shows how rapidly a new force can be fielded. Such a force can become an off-budget ally of the regulator, to extend the regulator's power and to shield the regulator from others (Congress, the executive or even old allies). A new force will be wanted when a better idea arises, to be sure. A new force will be wanted when a new idea arises, as well. Better or new, the idea and its development are dependent on the regulator.

CONCLUSION

We have argued that regulation responds to many interests, including the whim of the regulator. The past and present history of the SEC illustrates our case. That the SEC accomplishes no public good costs it no public support. Its rule by whim (short sells on the uptick, for example) leads many economists to explain its role, if not its birth, in terms of capture by the securities industry that it regulates. These economists know that stock exchange members did not benefit excessively from SEC regulation but they explain this fact by a model of many benefiting interests. These many interests models, however, miss an important part of the story, since they assume that the regulator is the faithful agent of someone or some group. Moreover, these models presume that an equilibrium exists. Regulation, as the story of the SEC shows, is characterized by change, both in beneficiaries and in benefits.

We have explained a systematic part of regulatory change as the product of strategies. We have attributed part of change to whim, that is, to the discretionary power of bureaucrats. We do not believe that "discretionary" implies "unpredictable." We do think it means prediction of ranges of outcomes, rather than prediction of unique outcomes, in politics.

---

[22] We agree that much of the pressure to move to a national marketing system results from institutional investors because of the advantages for these investors of a negotiated market over an auction market. See West and Tinic (1974) and Phillips (1978) for further discussions of this point.

ACKNOWLEDGMENT

We would like to thank Carolyn Weaver, Mike Murphy, and G. William Schwert for helpful comments on an earlier draft of this paper. We would also thank Richard Zecher and Susan Phillips for many fruitful discussions during the preparation of this paper and George Benston for his insightful discussion at the Conference. We, of course are responsible for any errors or lack of insights that remain.

REFERENCES

Aranson, P., and Ordeshook, P. A prolegomenon to a theory of the failure of representative democracy. Working Paper, Carnegie Mellon University, (1976).

Auster, R. The GPITPC and institutional entropy. *Public Choice*, Fall 1974, *19*, 77–83.

Barrett, M. The extent of disclosure in annual reports of large companies in seven countries. *The International Journal of Accounting*, Spring 1977, *12*, 1–25.

Barro, R. The control of politicians: An economic model, *Public Choice*, Spring 1972, *14*, 19–42.

Baxter, W. NYSE fixed commission rates: A private cartel goes public. *Stanford Law Review*, April 1970, *22*, 675–712.

Benston, G. *Corporate financial disclosure in the UK and the USA*, Lexington, Mass.: Lexington Books, 1976.

Benston, G. Required disclosure and the stock market: An evaluation of the Securities and Exchange Act of 1934. *American Economic Review*, March 1973, *63*, 132–155.

Benston, G. The effectiveness and effects of the SEC's accounting disclosure requirements, in H. G. Manne (Ed.), *Economic policy and the regulation of corporate securities,* Washington: American Enterprise Institute for Public Policy Research, 1969. (a)

Benston, G. The value of the SEC's accounting disclosure requirements. *Accounting Review*, July 1969, *44*, 515–32. (b)

Berle, A., and Means, G. *The modern corporation and private property.* New York: Commerce Clearing House, Inc., 1932.

Brock, W., and Magee, S. Equilibrium in political markets on pork-barrel issues. Report 7545, Center for Mathematical Studies in Business and Economics, University of Chicago (October 1975).

Buchanan, J., and Tullock, G. *The calculus of consent.* Ann Arbor: University of Michigan Press, 1962.

Buchanan, J. and Tideman, N. Gasoline Rationing and Market Pricing: Public Choice in Political Democracy. Research Paper No. 808231-1-12, Center for Study of Public Choice, Virginia Polytechnic Institute (January, 1974).

Bureau of the Census. *Historical statistics of the United States: Colonial Times to 1957.* Washington: U.S. Government Printing Office, 1961.

Bureau of the Census. *Historical statistics of the United States: Colonial times to 1970.* Washington: U.S. Government Printing Office, 1975.

Carey, J. *The rise of the accounting profession.* New York: American Institute of Certified Public Accountants, 1969.

Chatov, R. *Corporate financial reporting.* New York: Free Press, 1975.

Davis, L., and North, D. *Institutional change and American economic growth.* London: Cambridge University Press, 1971.

De Bedts, R. *The New Deal's SEC: The formative years.* New York: Columbia University Press, 1964.

Doede, R. The monopoly power of the New York Stock Exchange. Unpublished doctoral dissertation, University of Chicago, 1967.

Downs, A. *An Economic theory of democracy.* New York: Harper, 1957.

Eckert, R. On the incentives of regulators: The case of taxicabs. *Public Choice,* Spring 1973, *14,* 83-99.

Ehrlich, I., and Posner, R. An economic analysis of legal rule making. *Journal of Legal Studies,* January 1974, *3,* 257-86.

Friend, I. Economic foundations of stock market regulations. *Journal of Contemporary Business,* Summer 1976, *5,* 1-27.

Friend, I. and Blume, M. The consequences of competitive commissions on the New York Stock Exchange. Unpublished. University of Pennsylvania, April, 1972.

Friend, I., and Herman, E. The SEC through a glass darkly. *Journal of Business,* October 1964, *37,* 382-405.

Galbraith, J. *The great Crash of 1929.* Boston: Houghton Mifflin, 1955.

Goldin, K. Price externalities influence public policy. *Public Choice,* Fall 1975, *30,* 841-864.

Gonedes, N. Information production and capital market equilibrium. *Journal of Finance,* June 1975, *30,* 841-864.

Goodman, J. A theory of competitive regulatory equilibrium. Working Paper, Southern Methodist University, (1977).

Hirschleifer, J. Comment. *Journal of Law and Economics,* 1976, *19,* 241-44.

Hughes, J. *The governmental habit: Economic controls from Colonial times to the present.* New York: Basic Books, Inc., 1977.

Jaffe, J. The effect of regulation changes on insider trading. *The Bell Journal of Economics and Management Sciences,* Spring 1974, *5,* 93-121.

Jordan, W. Producer protection, prior market structure and the effects of government regulation. *Journal of Law and Economics,* April 1972, *15,* 151-76.

Kau, J., and Rubin, P. Self-interest, ideology, and logrolling in Congressional voting. Working Paper, University of Georgia.

Keynes, J. *The general theory of employment, interest, and money.* London: Macmillan and Co., 1936.

Kilko, G. *Railroads and regulation, 1877-1916.* Princeton: Princeton University Press, 1965.

Loss, L. *Securities regulation,* Vol. I. Boston: Little, Brown & Co., 1961.

Manne, H. G., ed. *Economic policy and the regulation of corporate securities.* Washington, D.C.: American Enterprise Institute, 1969.

McCormick, E. *Understanding the Securities Act and the SEC.* New York: American Book Co., 1948.

New York Stock Exchange, Inc. *Public transaction study:* 1976.

Niskanen, W., Jr. *Bureaucracy and representative government.* New York: Aldine Atherton, 1971.

Niskanen, W., Jr. Bureaucrats and politicians. *Journal of Law and Economics,* December 1975, *18,* 617-43.

Officer, R. The variability of the market factor of the New York Stock Exchange. *The Journal of Business,* July 1973, *46,* 434-453.

Olson, M. *The logic of collective action.* Cambridge: Harvard University Press, 1965.

Parrish, M. *Securities regulation and the New Deal.* New Haven: Yale University Press, 1970.

Pecora, F. *Wall Street under oath.* New York: Simon and Schuster, 1939.

Peltzman, S. Toward a more general theory of regulation. *Journal of Law and Economics,* August 1976, *19,* 211-40.

Phillips, S. Market structure and the trading of securities. Working Paper, Securities and Exchange Commission (February 1978).

Posner, R. The behavior of administrative agencies. *Journal of Legal Studies*, June 1972, Vol. *1*, 305-23. (a)
Posner, R. *Economics analysis of law*. New York: Little, Brown, 1972. (b)
Posner, R. Theories of economic regulation. *The Bell Journal of Economics and Management Science*, Autumn 1974, *2*, 335-58.
Reid, J., Jr. Understanding political events in the new economic history. *Journal of Economic History*, June 1977, *37*, 302-28.
Ripley, W. *Main Street and Wall Street*. Cambridge: Harvard University Press, 1926.
Schaefer, J., and Weiner, A. "Concentration trends and competition in the securities industry." *Financial Analysts Journal,* November/December 1977, *33,* 29-34.
Scholes, M. The market for securities: Substitution versus price pressure and the effects of information on shore prices. *The Journal of Business,* April 1972, *45*, 179-211.
Schwert, G. Public regulation of national securities exchanges: A test of the capture hypothesis. *The Bell Journal of Economics*, Autumn 1977a, *8*, 128-50.
Schwert, G. Stock exchange seats as capital assets. *The Journal of Financial Economics*, 1977b, *4*, 51-78.
Securities and Exchange Commission. *The effect of the absence of fixed rates of commission*, March 29, 1976.
Securities and Exchange Commission. *Institutional investor study report, summary volume.* Washington, D.C., March 1971.
Sommer, A., Jr. The other side. *Financial Executive,* May 1974, *42*, 36-39.
Stigler, G. Public regulation of the securities markets. *Journal of Business*, April 1964, *37*, 117-42.
Stigler, G. The theory of economic regulation. *The Bell Journal of Economics and Management Science*, Spring 1971, *2*, 3-21.
Stigler, G. Economic competition and political competition. *Public Choice*, Fall 1972, *13*, 91-106. (a)
Stigler, G. The process of economic regulation. *Antitrust Bulletin,* Spring 1972, *17*, 207-235. (b)
Stone, C. Blue sky laws and the 'hot issue' phenomenon: some preliminary evidence. Working Paper, California State University, Northridge, 1973.
Tullock, G. The paradox of revolution. *Public Choice,* Fall 1971, *16*, 89-99.
Wagner, R. Supply side aspects of the theory of local government: Owners, managers and take-over bids. Research Paper No. 527056-33-311, Center for Study of Public Choice, Virginia Polytechnic Institute, 1975.
Wagner, R. Pressure groups and political entrepreneurs: A review article. *Papers on Non-Market Decision Making*, 1966, *1*, 161-70.
Weaver, C. *The emergence, redirection and growth of social security: An interpretive history from a public choice perspective.* Doctoral dissertation, Virginia Polytechnic Institute and State University, 1977.
West, R., and Tinic, S. Institutionalization: Its impact on the provision of marketability services and the individual investor. *Journal of Contemporary Business*, Winter 1974, *3*, 24-47.

Discussion

GEORGE J. BENSTON

Professors Mackay and Reid have presented a useful and interesting review of theories (really, hypotheses) of regulation. To the four main theories—public interest or market failure, capture, many interests, and public choice—they add an additional variant, the self-interest of the regulator. As they recognize, the regulator's and all other participants' self-interest are present in all of the theories. Even the public interest theory can be stated to include the regulator's self-interest, since it can be defined to include the pleasure he gets from serving the public, punishing wrongdoers, being important, etc. Indeed, the self-interest of individuals may be said to underlie all theories of human behavior. It can explain just about everything and, therefore, the theorizer who emphasizes self-interest is in danger of lapsing into the familiar tautology that people only do that which pleasures them or they would not do it; hence whatever they do, they do for pleasure.

In general, when testing theories we often solve this problem by assigning many aspects of self-interest to "tastes and preferences," which then becomes (one hopes) a randomly distributed variable in a statistical association of the specified variables. However, this usual solution is difficult to apply to the present problem, since the researcher who wants to test theories of regulation is faced with the problem of very few cases to analyze. Indeed, the number of candidate explanatory variables far exceeds the number of observations. There is little scope, therefore, for analysts to determine empirically whether including variables that distinguish one theory from another would improve the explanatory power of the relationship, and hence be consistent or inconsistent with a given theory. Consequently, they are forced to rely on case studies in which one or another hypothesis occasionally can be rigorously tested, but which usually are descriptions spiced with ad hoc explanations. It is at this point that the temptation to tie up the loose ends with a self-interest explanation becomes difficult to resist, even at the expense of turning a theory into a tautology.

Among the theories of regulation, the public interest and capture theories are the least subject to the tautology trap. They only require a specification of the market failures which allegedly necessitated the regulations in question. For example, it is alleged that the financial statement disclosure requirements of the Securities Exchange Act of 1934 were necessitated by the failure of the market to provide the information required by investors for them to make informed investment decisions. To be sure, it is not easy to define operationally "information," "required by investors," and "informed investment decisions"; however such definitions can be constructed (such as defining the data that fulfill the Security Act's purposes as those required by the act and its associated regulations), and hypotheses can be drawn and tested. This is what I tried to do in several articles.[1] The capture hypothesis can be examined by considering the interests of those who promulgated and supported the legislation and the effect of the legislation on the wealth of those who were regulated. This is what William Schwert did. These hypotheses do not require a weighting of the strength of interests of diverse groups or a specification of the objective functions of regulators. The hypotheses also have other advantages. If it is true (as I suspect) that regulation often is enacted because the public and many legislators believe the market has failed and that regulation will correct perceived abuses to consumers, then tests of the public interest and capture hypotheses have direct public policy implications. If the tests indicate that the market had not failed and/or the regulators were captured, and if the public is informed effectively about the research findings, deregulation may follow. If deregulation is not enacted, the alternative hypotheses are supported. Therefore, it seems desireable to test the public interest and capture hypotheses first.

After delineating and describing these alternative regulation hypotheses, Professors Mackay and Reid turn their attention to the Securities and Exchange Commission (SEC). Their purpose is to determine how well the alternative theories of regulation "explain" its birth and evolution. For this purpose, they say

---

[1] For references, here and in following paragraphs, see Mackay and Reid.

that all of the hypotheses have merit. In particular, they accept the studies that indicate that the passage of the Securities Acts is not supported by the prior existence of market failure and that the public interest was not furthered by the SEC.[2] However, they criticize and find inconclusive William Schwert's test of the capture hypothesis, which indicates that brokers lost wealth as a consequence of the legislation as indicated by the price of stock exchange seats. I agree with their questioning of Schwert's conclusions in that he did not find an upward revision of seat prices when sections of the proposed Securities Exchange Act that would have adversely affected brokers and dealers were significantly weakened or dropped. However, I suggest that readers review Schwert's statistical work and compare it with Mackay and Reid's descriptive and graphical analysis. This comparison should show clearly that their criticisms and alternative analysis are not well drawn. Schwert's evidence, which is inconsistent with the capture hypothesis, essentially is conclusive, or at the very least, is superior to alternative tests of the hypothesis.

In any event, Mackay and Reid are concerned primarily with the "politicians and bureaucrats matter" hypothesis, which they put forth cogently and vigorously. Since I proposed a somewhat similar explanation of the behavior of a public regulatory agency in a book, *Corporate Financial Disclosure in the UK and the USA*, which appears to be not generally known to regulation theorists, I take the liberty of quoting the section entitled "Forces Governing the Behavior of a Public Regulatory Agency."

> In analysing the performance of an active administrative agency, such as the SEC, it is essential to remember that agencies are administered by people who are subject to the same sort of needs as are other people. They respond to rewards and punishments as much as do the accountants, directors, brokers, lawyers and bankers whose work they oversee. The factors that motivate the behavior of privately employed individuals are fairly obvious—long term personal gain in the form of monetary rewards (present and future), social status, personal pride, desire to see justice done, public reputation, personal security, etc. There is no reason to believe that employees and directors of public regulatory agencies are in general motivated differently, although they might value non-monetary rewards more than their counterparts in private industry. Naturally, public regulatory agency personnel may profess that they always put the public's interests before all else, and they may believe that they do so, but they are still self-interested human beings.
>
> Yet the public regulatory agency's mission may allow its employees to emphasize some non-pecuniary personal rewards. In particular, public regulatory agency officers may be attracted to that line of work because they are especially concerned to see

---

[2] They somewhat misdescribe my work. I was concerned primarily with testing the hypothesis that required disclosure provided investors with information as indicated by revaluations of the shares of the affected companies, not that the cost of disclosure was so great that it would result in downward revaluations of the shares. As all listed companies were affected by the regulations, I could not test the latter hypothesis with the data I used.

justice done and 'truth' prevail. Such would be the situation where the particular mission of the agency is believed to be the uncovering of falsehood and establishment of truth. Having discovered wrongdoing, many (perhaps most) people wish to see its perpetrators punished. Having searched for truth, many (again, perhaps most) people eventually claim to have found it and wish to see it proclaimed and adhered to. In most circumstances, wrongdoing must be proved in an adversary proceeding and truth cannot be imposed, but must be voluntarily accepted.[3] But, within the constraints of law, public opinion and private influence, the public regulatory agency is granted the power to punish wrongdoing and impose the truth. This power might be very appealing to persons who wish to serve the public and who believe that, without their help, the public (particularly its less informed and weaker members) would be ill-served.

Aside from these individual considerations, people's behaviour is affected primarily by the reward structure of their organisation. The employees of any organisation are rewarded for enhancing the utility of their supervisors who, in turn, are rewarded for enhancing institutional values. In private enterprise, the institutional values include maximisation of the wealth of the owners (some would say this is the only institutional value), which requires efficient production and distribution of goods and services to consumers.

A public agency, on the other hand, is not controlled by a market which dictates the aggregate level of services demanded by the public, but rather receives its funds through an imperfect political allocation system which at best attempts to tap societal demands for the public good. Public revenues are raised differentially from the various segments of society, usually on the basis of ability to pay and not on a basis consistent with the value of the benefits received from public expenditure. Hence the public agency usually seeks to maximise the quantity of the services it can provide, given its budget. Over time, the public administrator can only increase the level of his agency's services through larger budgets.

Consequently, the optimising behaviour of the public agency does not result in maximisation of net public benefit (or social welfare) in the way the profit maximising behaviour of a privately owned enterprise operating in a competitive market results in a Pareto optimum allocation of resources. The agency seeks rather to maximise the resources with which it can work—its budget. For some (perhaps most) agency directors, budget maximisation is a goal because only by this means can they maximise their own monetary rewards and prestige. For others, budget maximisation is desired so that they can better serve the public. Since the public generally does not pay for the services provided, the usual market constraint on production is not present. For the public agency, the constraint is the limited resources available to the legislature which must be allocated among competing agencies and other governmental functions. In seeking to maximise its budget, the public agency must be concerned with the government (legislature and executive) and with the part of the public that can influence the government. Thus its officers may not be able to prosecute the public good, as they see it, as zealously as they might like. On the other hand, the public agency is not as dependent upon brokers, companies and others whom it regulates as is a private regulatory agency, such as The (London) Stock Exchange.

Several hypotheses about the behaviour of public regulatory agencies can be

---

[3] An exception is the temporary ability of teachers to impose their views on students. The students, though, soon pass out of the school. The regulated must leave the industry to achieve a similar freedom.

drawn from this analysis. First, a public regulatory agency will tend to serve organised and relatively enduring groups (who can serve as lobbyists in the political process of securing larger agency budgets) rather than the diverse, unorganised general public. However, the agency may also act zealously to serve the public, should its officers feel this need strongly and should other factors allow this action. Secondly, the agency will act to expand and rarely to contract the scope of its operations. Thirdly, the agency will seek to avoid scandals and situations which might cause the general public and other government officials to conclude that it is not 'doing its job,' and consequently to question future budgets. Hence the agency avoids risks and institutes formal rules that prevent someone from blaming a specific person for an error of judgement [George J. Benston, *Corporate Financial Disclosure in the UK and the USA*, Lexington, Ma: Lexington Books–D. C. Heath, 1976. Pp. 167-169. Reprinted with permission of the author.

Since my structuring of the "public officials" matter hypothesis is similar to theirs, I cannot be too critical of them. However, I should note that they have not really tested their hypothesis as I had hoped they would. In particular, they suggest that zealots dominate the ranks of would-be regulators. Yet they do not identify the zealots who were the movers and draftsmen of the Securities Acts and whether or not they found their rewards as employed regulators. (My reading of secondary sources, particularly DeBedts and Parish, does not generally support their otherwise plausible hypothesis.) They then suggest that successive regulators will be concerned with preserving and enlarging their possibilities for exercising discretion, but they present no evidence on this question, nor do they explain the casual observation that the SEC's bureaucrats limited their discretionary actions until relatively recently. This recent explosion of activity by the SEC, in which it opposed the stock exchanges' price fixing rules, promulgated accounting requirements, and over-ruled the professional accounting establishment to whom it had delegated authority, also is unexplained.

The problem, which I believe they recognize, is that even were such explanations attempted, it is difficult for the researcher to avoid the charge of ad hoc reasoning. Nevertheless, each description and analysis of agency history and behavior adds to our knowledge. Perhaps eventually we will have enough such studies to permit a generalized hypothesis to be tested on new data.

Chapter 7

Taxes, Transfers, and Income Inequality

EDGAR K. BROWNING and WILLIAM R. JOHNSON

Certainly one of the most significant legacies of the New Deal era is the welfare state we live in today. Many familiar social welfare programs have their origin in the Roosevelt years. Social security, unemployment insurance, public housing, a temporary food subsidy, and various public works programs were enacted during this period. Moreover, the federal government encouraged states to assist in the effort to help the needy through the use of matching grants to provide " . . . assistance to the needy aged, the needy blind, and to children under sixteen deprived of parental support; and also grants for the establishment of maternal and child-health services, medical, and other services for the care of homeless, dependent, and neglected children" (Hacker, 1949).

Prior to the 1930s, total federal expenditures seldom exceeded 5% of the national income, and only a fraction of total outlays was devoted to social welfare objectives. By 1976, federal expenditures on social welfare programs alone equaled 14% of the national income. Much of this growth has occurred since World War II; in 1947, the federal government was spending only 5% of the national income on social welfare programs. Nonetheless, the New Deal era marked the beginning of an expanding role for government in this area, an expansion which continues today.

Many of the programs enacted during the Roosevelt era were viewed as temporary programs which were designed to relieve distress during the depression rather than as permanent mechanisms to redistribute income during more normal times. However, today these programs, and their modern variations, accomplish a massive redistribution of income, and this has come to represent a major modern rationalization for their continuation and expansion. As noted in *Business Week* (1975), " . . . the greatest single force changing and expanding the role of the federal government in the United States today is the push for equality." Perhaps this political force is simply the inevitable outgrowth of the change in attitudes that is widely believed to have been set in motion during the New Deal. As Henry Steele Commager (1949) noted in writing about the New Deal in 1945: "More important than bare relief, was the acceptance of the principle of the responsibility of the state for the welfare and security of its people—for employment, health and general welfare."

It is our purpose to examine how government social welfare expenditures and the taxes that finance them have altered the distribution of income in the United States today. After a brief discussion of the data used in this study (pp. 130-132), we examine the distribution of the tax burden by income class (pp. 132-137). A discussion of the combined effect of taxes and transfers on the income distribution appears on pages 137-141. Finally we appraise the degree of income inequality that remains after taxes and transfers have been taken into account (pp. 142-148). Our major conclusion is that, partly as a result of taxes and transfers, the distribution of income is substantially less unequal than is commonly believed.

DESCRIPTION OF DATA

The data used in this chapter are from the March 1975 Current Population Survey (CPS) which collected information on 1974 money income and household characteristics for a national sample of about 50,000 households. The data was subsequently updated to correspond to 1976 levels. Income from important cash and in-kind transfer programs was then imputed to the sample by the Mathematica Policy Research under contract to the Congressional Budget Office.[1] The imputation procedure is complicated but was essentially based on a comparison of the household's characteristics with the requirements of the particular transfer program. An important feature of the imputation method is that it ac-

---

[1] We are grateful to John Korbel of the Congressional Budget Office for making the augmented CPS file available to us.

counts for the fact that fewer households than are legally entitled participate in most transfer programs. As a consequence, total imputed transfer benefits for the sample are consistent with national expenditures on the programs.

Despite the wealth of information of this augmented CPS data file, further imputations and assumptions had to be made before the estimates in this chapter could be computed. These imputations involve both income and tax rates.

Income

Capital income for the household was deemed to be the sum of interest received, rents, the household's share of corporate profits, capital share of proprietor's income,[2] and private pension income. The household's share of corporate profits is estimated by making the common assumption that retained earnings of corporations flow to households (presumably as capital gains on equities) in proportion to each household's receipt of dividends.[3]

The treatment of private pension receipts as capital income is a more controversial assumption. Ideally, we would like to measure the return to accumulated pension savings in the year it was earned rather than the year it was disbursed, but this is impossible with our data. Treating pensions as income in the year received is a necessary assumption, but one which has the virtue of mitigating to some extent the annual income versus lifetime income problems in measures of income distribution. Counting all of the pension as income rather than dissaving is not too serious a problem since: (*a*) most of the disbursement will be accumulated interest; and (*b*) the employer contribution to the pension is not counted as income in the year it is made. Any biases this assumption imparts are likely to make the tax system appear less progressive since the tax rate on low income retirees will go up.

Transfer income includes most cash transfer programs, government pensions, veterans' benefits, social insurance benefits, and the most important in-kind transfers.

Labor income includes the employee and employer contributions to social insurance funds. Finally, under the incidence assumptions of the paper, before-tax labor and capital income include indirect taxes (sales and excise taxes) which are imputed evenly to both types of factor incomes.

Taxes

Only state and federal income taxes and social security taxes are explicitly listed in the augmented CPS data file. The following imputations were added:

[2] Capital share was estimated as in Pechman and Okner (1974).
[3] The ratio of retained earnings to dividends was taken for the 5-year period 1972–76 to avoid the peculiarities of one particular year.

1. Unemployment insurance taxes were approximated as 2% of the first $4000 of wage income. While not precisely accurate for every state, the formula conforms generally to the national system (Facts and Figures on Government Finance, 1977).

2. Taxes on capital are assumed to apply at the same rate to all forms of capital income. Hence, an average capital tax rate can be calculated by dividing aggregate taxes on capital by aggregate capital income. Capital taxes include corporate income taxes and property taxes. Capital income includes the capital share of proprietor's income, corporate profits, interest received, and the rental income of persons (including the imputed income from homeownership) (Economic Report of the President, 1978). The average rate of tax on capital income was computed to be 42.7%.

3. Sales and excise taxes include federal excise taxes, customs duties, and state and local sales and gross receipts taxes (Economic Report of the President, 1978). The indirect tax rate on gross factor income was estimated to be 6%.

Omissions

Although the adjusted data base represents a more comprehensive measure of income than that commonly used, there are still some notable omissions. We have allocated $200 billion in cash and in-kind transfers among households, but in 1976 federal and state-local government expenditures on social welfare programs totalled $331 billion. The major expenditure program with benefits not allocated as income was public education, on which $86 billion was spent in 1976. The remaining $45 billion in social welfare expenditures that was not imputed to households represents a multitude of relatively small programs. In addition, no attempt has been made to impute the benefits of general expenditure programs (such as national defense) to households.

Thus, while we estimate the distribution of all taxes among households, only those government expenditures on major cash and in-kind programs are counted as benefits to households.

THE TAX SYSTEM

How tax burdens are distributed by income class is a topic of perennial interest in the field of public finance. If the tax system results in tax burdens that are the same percent of income for all income classes, the relative distribution of income would be unchanged. This is what most tax experts believe to be the case (Pechman and Okner, 1974; Musgrave *et al.*, 1974). The major reason for this belief is that taxes thought to fall on households in proportion to consumption outlays (such as sales and excise taxes) are estimated as highly regressive. These taxes tend to offset the progressive impact of taxes such as the federal income tax, yielding an overall tax system that is roughly proportional to income. While the exact distribution of tax burdens does depend, to a degree, on what incidence assumptions are employed for certain taxes, most economists have felt comfortable with the generalization that the tax system is proportional.

It has recently been argued (Browning, 1978) that there is a major theoretical error in the conventional tax incidence analysis underlying estimates of tax burdens by income class. The error lies in allocating the burden of a tax in proportion to consumption of the taxed product or products, as is done with sales and excise taxes. To understand this issue most easily, consider a general sales tax levied at the same rate on all goods and services. The exact effects of this tax depend on whether absolute product prices are assumed to be affected. Two polar outcomes are conceivable. First, product prices could rise by the amount of the tax, leaving factor incomes (labor income and capital income) unchanged in nominal terms. Second, product prices could remain unchanged with a reduction in factor incomes in proportion to the size of the tax.

These two outcomes appear to be the same in real terms: In both cases factor prices have fallen relative to product prices. If we abstract from differences in the percentage of income saved, it would seem that we could allocate tax burdens either in proportion to total consumption outlays or in proportion to factor income: Both procedures would yield the same result. This is the theoretical basis for allocating the burden of the sales tax in proportion to consumption outlays.

The problem with this analysis arises when we recognize that households derive income not only from supplying labor and capital, but also in the form of government transfer payments. Consider a household whose entire income is in the form of a transfer payment. If a sales tax leads to a higher price level, and the money value of the transfer is unchanged, then the household bears a tax burden because the real value of its income falls. On the other hand, if the price level is unaffected, this household would bear no burden at all. Once transfer payments are incorporated into the analysis, it is important whether or not taxes raise the price level.

Under certain assumptions, it could still be argued that the burden of a general sales tax should be allocated in proportion to consumption outlays. The required conditions are, however, highly restrictive and implausible. It must be assumed that the price level rises *exactly* in proportion to the size of the tax *and* that the money value of transfers is unchanged. Both of these assumptions are subject to serious question, especially the latter. Under existing legislation, several transfer programs automatically vary transfers in proportion to the price level (as measured by the consumer price index). This is true, for example, of the single most important transfer program, social security. In addition, the money

TABLE 7.1
Sources of Before-Tax–After-Transfer Income of Households[a]

Lowest to highest income groups in quintiles	Labor share (%)	Capital share (%)	Transfer share (%)
First	30.7	6.7	62.6
Second	57.3	8.5	34.2
Third	76.2	8.1	15.7
Fourth	82.0	8.9	9.1
Fifth	64.0	31.0	5.0

[a] Households ranked by before-tax–after-transfer household income.

value of all in-kind transfers automatically rises when the prices of the subsidized goods rise. Moreover, even for transfers that are not explicitly linked to consumer prices, it appears likely that legislatures make ad hoc adjustments in transfer payments in response to any changes in the price level.

These observations lead us to assume that the real value of transfers is unaffected by changes in the tax system. Granting this assumption, how should the burden of a general sales tax be allocated? The answer is that it should be allocated in proportion to factor income. Thus, if a sales tax raises revenue equal to 5% of total factor income, a household whose entire income is factor income bears a burden equal to 5% of its income. A household with half of its income as transfers would bear a burden equal to 2.5% of its total income since its factor income falls by 5% and because factor income is only half of total income. This method of allocating the burden of a sales tax is correct regardless of what happens to the price level as long as we assume the real value of transfers is fixed. Excise taxes should also be allocated in this way.

Whether sales and excise taxes are regressive or progressive therefore depends on the proportion of total income received as transfers in the various income classes. Table 7.1 gives the transfer, labor, and capital shares of total income received by each quintile of households. As would be expected, transfers are a very high percentage of total income in the lowest quintile, and this percentage falls steadily as we move up the income distribution. This means that sales and excise taxes are really progressive taxes; they fall in proportion to factor income, and factor income is a much smaller percentage of total income for the bottom quintile than for the top.

Having explained the proper treatment of sales and excise taxes, let us now turn to a consideration of the incidence of all taxes together. The methods used to allocate the burdens of other taxes are based on a competitive model in which the total supplies of labor and capital are assumed to be uanaffected by taxes. Under these conditions, payroll taxes are borne by workers in proportion to covered earnings, personal income taxes are borne by the individuals, and corpo-

TABLE 7.2.
Average Tax Rates by Quintiles of Households[a]
(percentages)

Lowest to highest income groups in quintiles	Sales and excises	Payroll	Income	Corporate and property	Total
First	2.1	4.2	1.6	2.7	10.7
Second	3.7	6.5	4.2	3.4	17.8
Third	4.8	8.5	7.5	3.3	24.0
Fourth	5.2	8.2	10.4	3.6	27.3
Fifth	5.4	5.0	13.2	12.5	36.1

[a] Households ranked by before-tax–after-transfer household income. Average tax rates are the total tax burden divided by the total before-tax–after-transfer income.

rate and property taxes are borne in proportion to capital income (see Chapter 3 of Pechman and Okner, 1974).

Table 7.2 shows the results of calculations based on these incidence assumptions. Sales and excise taxes are progressive, as expected, rising steadily from an average tax rate of 2.1% for the lowest quintile to a rate of 5.4% at the top. The average tax rate of payroll taxes (primarily the social security tax) rises up to the third quintile, drops slightly for the fourth quintile and then more sharply for the highest quintile. This pattern of rates at the bottom of the distribution reflects the fact that payroll taxes fall on labor income, and labor income is a smaller percentage of total income at the bottom (see Table 7.1). The lower rate at the top reflects the ceiling on taxable earnings of the social security tax together with the smaller share of labor income in the top quintile.

The pattern of rates under personal income taxes (both federal and state) comes as no surprise since these taxes are levied at highly graduated rates. Of course, since these rates relate taxes to total incomes, they show that, despite tax "loopholes," higher income classes bear a much heavier tax rate than lower income classes. Finally, the corporate and property taxes are also progressive. Since these taxes have been allocated in proportion to total capital income, their progressivity is due strictly to the fact that capital income is a higher percentage of total income in higher income classes (see Table 7.1).

Since each category of taxes is separately progressive through most or all of the income distribution, the total tax system is highly progressive, as shown in the last column. Tax rates rise steadily from 10.7% for the bottom quintile to 36.1% for the top quintile. The top quintile alone pays 58% of all taxes! At the other extreme, the bottom quintile pays 1.6% of all taxes. The average tax burden per household in the top quintile is $16,672; the comparable figure for the lowest quintile is $428.

These figures contrast sharply with all earlier estimates of tax burdens by in-

TABLE 7.3
Effect of Tax System on Distribution of Income[a]

Lowest to highest income groups in quintiles	Total income ($ billion)		Share of income (%)	
	Before-tax	After-tax	Before-tax	After-tax
First	65.5	58.4	4.3	5.4
Second	153.4	126.2	10.0	11.6
Third	239.2	181.6	15.5	16.7
Fourth	349.0	253.8	22.7	23.3
Fifth	733.2	468.4	47.6	43.0

[a] Households ranked by before-tax–after-transfer household income.

come class by displaying a far greater degree of progressivity. The major reason for this difference is our treatment of sales and excise taxes. If our analysis of the incidence of these taxes is correct, there is no doubt that the tax system is highly progressive. It might also be added that the degree of progressivity is virtually unaffected by employing alternative incidence assumptions for the corporate, property, and (employer portion of) payroll taxes (Browning, 1978).

A progressive tax system implies that the after-tax distribution of income is more equal than the before-tax distribution. Table 7.3 shows how the tax system affects the share of income received by each quintile. Before taxes, the bottom quintile receives 4.3% of total before-tax income; after taxes, it receives 5.4% of total income. The share of the top quintile drops from 47.6% to 43%. Note that the relative position of every quintile except the top one is improved by the tax system. This is because the average rate of tax for the four lowest quintiles is lower than the national average rate of 29.3%. Only the top quintile pays more than the average rate of tax.

Our first reaction to the estimates in Table 7.3 was surprise at how modest an equalizing effect the tax system had on the distribution of income. Upon reflection, however, taxes do seem to make a significant contribution toward equalizing income. Note that the ratio of incomes in the top quintile to incomes in the bottom quintile is eleven-to-one before taxes, but only eight-to-one after taxes. Surely, that constitutes a major change. Another way of looking at this matter is to consider the maximum contribution the tax system could make to improving the position of the bottom quintile. This maximum contribution would be made, of course, if the tax system placed a zero burden on the lowest quintile. In that event, the share of after-tax income for the lowest quintile would only be 6.0%. Since the actual tax system increases the share from 4.3% to 5.4%, it improves the position of the lowest quintile by two-thirds as much as the most progressive tax system conceivable.

Nonetheless, it remains true that the contribution of the tax system by itself to equalizing incomes is inherently limited. The tax system cannot increase the absolute incomes of low income households; at best, it can only avoid reducing income further. Government transfers, on the other hand, are capable of raising incomes. To appreciate fully the extent to which government influences the distribution of income, it is necessary to consider how taxes and transfers together redistribute income. That topic is considered in the following section.

TAXES AND TRANSFERS

Taxes and transfers together effect an enormous redistribution of income. Table 7.4 documents this impact by showing separately the cash transfers, in-kind transfers, and taxes for each quintile. In this table, households are ranked on the basis of their incomes before taxes and transfers. As we will see later, the way in which households are ranked has a surprisingly large influence on the measure of redistribution and income inequality.

Table 7.4 suggests that taxes and transfers together accomplish a massive redistribution of income in favor of low income households. The bottom quintile received a total of $82.0 billion in cash and in-kind transfers and paid a total of $3.2 billion in taxes, for a net transfer in its favor of $78.8 billion. This net transfer amounts to $2775 per person in the lowest quintile. Since the official poverty line is about $2700 for a single person household, and somewhat less per person for multi-person households, this net transfer is more than sufficient to raise every household above its poverty line. That official poverty statistics still record some 25 million persons in poverty in 1976 reflect primarily the fact that in-kind transfers are not counted as income.[4]

The second quintile predictably received a smaller net transfer. It received $49.1 billion in cash and in-kind transfers and paid $28.0 billion in taxes for a net transfer of $21.1 billion. This net transfer amounts to $588 per person in the second quintile. The lowest two quintiles together received a net transfer of $99.9 billion, more than the total amount ($93 billion) spent on national defense. At the other extreme, the top two quintiles received cash and in-kind transfers of $41.7 billion and paid taxes of $360.8 billion, a net transfer away from these groups of $319.1 billion. Of this, $242.3 billion is a net transfer from the highest quintile alone.

It should be mentioned here that these estimated net transfers do not reflect fully the effect of taxes and government expenditures on the distribution of in-

---

[4] Another reason is that, while the average transfer may be sufficient to raise every family above its poverty line, some families receive transfers well below the average and therefore remain below their poverty lines. Recent studies have estimated that the inclusion of in-kind transfers as income would reduce the number of persons with incomes below their poverty lines by 50% to 75%.

TABLE 7.4
Taxes, Transfers, and Income by Income Class ($ in billions)[a]

Lowest to highest income groups in quintiles	Before-tax–Before-transfer income	Cash transfers	In-kind transfers	Taxes	After-tax–After-transfer income	% Share of income	
						Before-tax–Before-transfer	After-tax After-transfer
First	5.7	60.4	21.6	3.2	84.4	0.4	7.8
Second	99.0	38.9	10.2	28.0	120.1	7.4	11.0
Third	209.4	23.2	4.2	59.2	176.8	15.6	16.2
Fourth	321.8	17.1	2.3	96.2	245.1	24.0	22.5
Fifth	704.8	19.8	2.5	264.6	462.4	52.6	42.5

[a] Households ranked by before-tax–before-transfer household income.

come. While we are allocating all taxes, only certain transfers and not all government expenditures are allocated among the income classes. Total taxes allocated here are $451.2 billion and total transfers allocated are $200.2 billion. Thus, the average net transfer across all households is negative in this tabulation. To put this point somewhat differently, not only do the lowest two quintiles receive transfers $99.9 billion greater than the total taxes they pay, they also receive services from government expenditures on schools, highways, national defense, and the like, that are not included in these estimates.

The last two columns in Table 7.4 show the striking contrast in the relative distribution of income before taxes and transfers and after taxes and transfers. Before taxes and transfers, the income of the top quintile is 131 times as great as the bottom quintile, while after tax and transfers, the income of the top quintile is only 5.4 times as great. It is tempting to conclude that the tax-transfer system has had a major effect in reducing income inequality. This may not be the case. The distribution referred to as "before taxes and transfers" is not the distribution that would prevail in the absence of these government transfer programs. Instead, this distribution simply shows the factor incomes of households after they have responded to the tax-transfer system. For example, the very low factor incomes of the lowest quintiles may be due to a reduction in labor supply and saving by low income households in response to the high marginal tax rates of the tax-transfer system. In short, taxes and transfers may make the *realized* before tax and transfer distribution more unequal. If so, the difference in the distribution in Table 7.4 overstates the equalizing effect of government on the distribution of income.

It may have been noted that the percentage shares shown in the last column of Table 7.4, depicting the after tax and transfer distribution, differ from those shown in Table 7.3. This difference is due solely to the way households are ranked. In Table 7.3, households were ranked by their before-tax–after-transfer incomes, while in Table 7.4, they were ranked by their before-tax–before-transfer incomes. As it turns out, this seemingly minor difference has a major effect on the degree of measured income inequality after taxes and transfers.

Table 7.5 presents the same information as Table 7.4, but with households ranked on the basis of their before-tax–after-transfer incomes. A number of differences stand out. The before tax and transfer distribution is not greatly different except for the lowest quintile; it receives more than four times as much factor income when compared to the previous ranking. The net transfer in favor of the lowest quintile is much smaller on this ranking, $34.2 billion instead of $78.8 billion. Finally, note that the final distribution after taxes and transfers is significantly more unequal. In particular, the share of the lowest quintile is now 5.4%, 30% lower than the estimated share when households are ranked according to their factor incomes.

As mentioned above, we found these large differences surprising. Apparently,

TABLE 7.5
Taxes, Transfers, and Income by Income Class: Alternative Ranking ($ in billions)[a]

Lowest to highest income groups in quintiles	Before-tax–Before-transfer income	Cash transfers	In-kind transfers	Taxes	After-tax–After-transfer income	% Share of income Before-tax–Before-transfer	% Share of income After-tax After-transfer
First	24.6	29.2	11.8	6.8	58.8	1.8	5.4
Second	101.1	38.5	13.8	27.1	126.3	7.5	11.6
Third	201.8	30.8	6.6	57.5	181.7	15.0	16.7
Fourth	317.1	28.1	4.2	95.6	253.8	23.6	23.3
Fifth	696.6	33.0	4.0	265.1	468.5	51.9	43.0

[a] Households ranked by before-tax–after-transfer household income.

government transfers alter the relative positions of households, especially those at the bottom of the income distribution, to a major degree. Ignoring differences in family size among households, this could not happen if transfers were made through a negative income tax. A negative income tax would leave the relative ranking of households completely unchanged, and this is sometimes cited as an advantage of this kind of program. (If all transfers were made through a negative income tax, tables constructed like Table 7.4 and 7.5 would be identical.)

An example may help to clarify what factors give rise to the differences between Tables 7.4 and 7.5. Consider two households: one an elderly couple whose only income is a social security pension of $4000, and the other, a non-aged couple whose only income is earnings of $3000. Ranked by before-tax-before-transfer income, the aged couple is in the bottom quintile with a zero factor income while the non-aged couple is in the second quintile, with a factor income of $3000. On this ranking, the social security pension shows up as a large net transfer to the lowest quintile. However when ranked by before-tax-after-transfer income, the non-aged couple is ranked in the lowest quintile while the aged couple is in the second quintile. Under this ranking, factor income is higher than before in the bottom quintile ($3000 instead of zero), transfers are lower (zero instead of $4000), and after-tax-after-transfer is lower. It is this type of shifting in the positions of households in the income distribution that produces the differences between Tables 7.4 and 7.5. From the magnitudes shown in the tables, it is clear that transfers alter the relative positions of households to a major degree.

The significance of this reranking caused by government transfers remains to be considered. Specifically, does Table 7.4 or 7.5 represent a better picture of the way the government affects the distribution of income? It seems to us that both tables present pertinent information and that the choice between them may depend largely on the questions being investigated. For example, if our interest is in how government affects those households that are poorest in terms of their factor incomes, then Table 7.4 is the logical choice. If our concern is with the degree of inequality after taxes and transfers, Table 7.5 may be more relevant. Table 7.5, on the other hand, tends to obscure the amount of redistribution that is actually occurring. Table 7.5 contains within a given quintile quite dissimilar households; some with large transfers (low taxes) and other households with similar after-transfer incomes but with low transfers (and hence higher taxes). The net result is that there is a significant redistribution *within* the quintiles, especially the lower ones, when ranked as in Table 7.5. Finally, while Table 7.5 gives the more accurate picture of the actual final after-tax-after-transfer distribution, Table 7.4 is a better indication of the potential equalizing effect of existing taxes and transfers *if* transfers were targeted more carefully so as to avoid altering the relative positions of households so greatly.

EVALUATING INCOME INEQUALITY

Tables 7.4 and 7.5 present estimates of the after-tax–after-transfer distribution of income among households. It is tempting to interpret these estimates as measures of the degree of income inequality, and frequently such numbers are interpreted in this way. Such an interpretation would be plausible if households were alike in all relevant respects except for differences in after-tax–after-transfer income. Unfortunately, this is not so; there are some striking differences among the households that occupy the various quintiles.

Table 7.6 shows the variation in the number of persons and quantities of labor supplied among quintiles for the two rankings we are using. Although each quintile contains the same number of households, the number of persons per household varies. Generally speaking, lower-income households contain fewer persons. Average household size on the before-tax–after-transfer ranking is 1.6 persons for the lowest quintile and rises steadily until it reaches 3.3 persons for the highest quintile. Thus, while the top quintile receives eight times as much after-tax–after-transfer income as the bottom quintile, this higher income is supporting twice as many persons.

Labor supply (and its converse, leisure consumed) also varies systematically among the quintiles. Total hours of work rise sharply as we move up the income distribution. The variation in hours of work per adult is somewhat less since there are fewer adults in the lower quintiles, but even so the average adult in the top quintile works three times as much as the average adult in the bottom quintile. (These differences can most easily be understood as reflecting the different types of family units in the quintiles. Six out of seven households in the lowest quintile are either single person households, female-headed households with children, or elderly households. By contrast, nine out of ten households in the top quintile are non-elderly, multiperson households.)

It seems clear that ignoring these differences in households leads to an overstatement of the degree of inequality in relative standards of living. The difficult issue is exactly how to adjust the estimates in Tables 7.4 and 7.5 to take account of differences in family size and amount of leisure. The following two adjustments are made: (*a*) differences in family size are taken into account by using per capita family income, and (*b*) differences in leisure time are evaluated by estimates of foregone wages in assessing the real income position of different individuals. A detailed discussion of the issues involved in making these adjustments is presented in the Appendix.

Now let us turn to the empirical estimates of the impact of adjusting for differences in family size and leisure. We will make use of the following three methods of ranking households in terms of their incomes:

Ranking A: Households ranked by before-tax–after-transfer household income.

TABLE 7.6
Distributions of Hours of Work and Persons

Lowest to highest income groups in quintiles	Before-tax–Before-transfer ranking			Before-tax–After-tranfer ranking		
	Number of persons (millions)	Hours of work (billions)	Hours of work per adult (hours per year)	Number of persons (millions)	Hours of work (billions)	Hours of work per adult (hours per year)
First	28.4	3.2	155	25.3	8.0	404
Second	35.9	16.4	643	37.3	16.7	660
Third	43.2	29.6	1007	45.4	28.0	940
Fourth	50.2	39.1	1207	50.0	37.2	1131
Fifth	52.4	47.0	1270	52.1	45.2	1205

Ranking B: Households ranked by before-tax–before-transfer per capita household income.

Ranking C: Households ranked by after-tax–after-transfer per capita household income.

It will be noted that Ranking A is the same as the one employed in Tables 7.1-7.3 and Table 7.5 earlier. Ranking B is analogous to that used in Table 7.4, except that here we placed households with the lowest per person factor incomes (households before-tax–before-transfer income divided by the number of household members) at the bottom. Ranking C is the same as B except that it uses after-tax-after-transfer per capita incomes.

Table 7.7 presents the results of this adjustment. In all cases the quintiles in Table 7.7 now contain 20% of the population, not 20% of households (as in previous tables). Consider the first two columns, giving the before-tax–before-transfer and after-tax–after-transfer income shares using Ranking A. When we used the same ranking method in Table 7.5, we reported that the poorest 20% of households receive 5.4% of total after tax and transfer income, but that these households contained less than 20% of the population. Now it can be seen that the poorest households containing 20% of the population receive 10.4% of final income, while the wealthiest families containing 20% of the population receive 37.4% of final income. These figures suggest less inequality than the distributions based on 20% of households.

The problem with these figures is that the criterion used to rank households (household income) is different than the criterion used to define quintiles (20% of the population—implicitly identifying per capita household income as relevant). Nonetheless, these figures are of interest because they indicate that the *specific* households identified as being poorest in conventional statistics (which rank in terms of household income regardless of household size) are significantly better off in terms of their per capita incomes.

Ranking B and C are consistent since per capita incomes are used to rank households and since the quintiles contain 20% of the population. Under Ranking B, the 20% of the population with the lowest before-tax–before-transfer per capita income receive 1.6% of total family income, but these same persons receive 9.9% of total after tax and transfer income. Clearly, the tax and transfer system redistributes a large amount of income in favor of households with the lowest per capita incomes. In absolute terms, the total factor income of the lowest quintile is $21.4 billion, but after taxes and transfers its total income is $107.7 billion—a net redistribution in its favor of $86.3 billion ($2030 per person).

Just as we noted with Tables 7.4 and 7.5, the effect of transfers and taxes is to produce a very different ranking of households. This is shown in Table 7.7 by the differences between the income shares under Rankings B and C. Under Ranking C, the final share of the lowest quintile is 6.2%, rather than 9.9% under

TABLE 7.7
Distribution of Income by Quintiles of Persons (Percentage Shares)

Lowest to highest income groups in quintiles	Ranking A		Ranking B		Ranking C	
	Before-tax- Before-transfer	After-tax- After-transfer	Before-tax- Before-transfer	After-tax- After-transfer	Before-tax- Before-transfer	After-tax- After-transfer
First	4.5	10.4	1.6	9.9	4.3	6.2
Second	11.0	14.0	8.8	11.2	9.7	11.4
Third	16.3	16.8	14.5	14.9	14.4	15.8
Fourth	22.2	21.4	22.0	21.0	21.0	22.2
Fifth	45.9	37.4	53.2	43.0	50.6	44.4

Ranking B. Apparently, many of those households that have the lowest before-tax-before-transfer per capita incomes (Ranking B) receive such large transfers that they are no longer in the bottom quintile when ranked on the basis of after-tax-after-transfer per capita incomes. The final degree of income inequality (excluding the leisure adjustment) is probably best indicated by the after-tax-after-transfer distribution under Ranking C, if we think per capita household income is the appropriate index of economic standards of living. At the same time, Ranking B probably gives a better picture of how government tax and transfer policies benefit those with the lowest per capita incomes. Again, we find it surprising how greatly the after-tax-after-transfer share of income of the bottom quintile differs under these two rankings (just as it did in Tables 7.4 and 7.5).

Now we can incorporate the estimated value of leisure into the distributions. Table 7.8 is the same as Table 7.7 except that the estimated value of leisure has been added to the total income of each quintile. (The rankings in Table 7.8 are the same as in Table 7.7; households are not ranked on the basis of their income including leisure. Since the leisure adjustment was based on group data, we felt that the estimates for specific households were too imprecise to utilize in ranking households.) The total value of leisure time, calculated on the assumption that each adult could work a maximum of 2000 hours per year, was estimated at $911 billion. This is clearly a very large adjustment since it increases total before-tax-before-transfer income by 68% (from $1340 billion to $2251 billion) and total after-tax-after-transfer income by 84% (from $1089 billion to $2000 billion).

The inclusion of leisure makes all of the distributions, before taxes and transfers as well as after taxes and transfers, decidedly more equal. This reflects the wide variation in hours of work that was reported earlier. Even though the relative distributions become more equal, the absolute differences between incomes at the top and bottom are widened. For example, the value of leisure for the bottom quintile under Ranking B was estimated at $123 billion, while it was $244 billion for the top quintile. (Although the lowest quintile consumes much more leisure, the wage rate used to estimate its value is less than one-fifth the wage rate for the top quintile.)

As already pointed out, Ranking C probably provides the best estimate of the degree of final income inequality. After all of our adjustments, the bottom quintile under this ranking receives 9.1% of income, while the top quintile receives 37.3%, about four times as much. This can be contrasted with figures commonly used to represent the extent of income inequality. For example, using household money incomes (unadjusted for in-kind transfers or differences in family size) before payment of direct taxes, the Bureau of the Census has estimated that the share of the bottom quintile in 1974 was 3.8% while the share of the top quintile was 44.4%, about 12 times as great.

One final issue deserves mention. None of our figures include any estimates of

TABLE 7.8
Distribution of Income (Including Leisure) by Quintiles of Persons (Percentage Shares)

Lowest to highest income groups in quintiles	Ranking A		Ranking B		Ranking C	
	Before-tax–Before-transfer	After-tax–After-transfer	Before-tax–Before-transfer	After-tax–After-transfer	Before-tax–Before-transfer	After-tax–After-transfer
First	9.3	13.0	6.5	11.6	7.6	9.1
Second	13.8	15.7	12.6	14.4	12.2	13.4
Third	17.3	17.7	16.3	16.8	16.4	17.4
Fourth	21.3	20.8	22.1	21.6	22.0	22.8
Fifth	38.3	32.7	42.4	35.6	41.8	37.3

the benefits from expenditures on public education. It turns out that this omission is of some importance under the per capita ranking. Under Ranking C, for example, the bottom quintile contains 16.4 million school age children (between the ages of 5 and 18), while the top quintile contains only 3.9 million school age children. (When ranked in this way, households at the bottom are of larger than average size, while those at the top are of smaller than average size—the opposite of normal household rankings.) If educational expenditures are allocated in proportion to the number of school age children, the share of the bottom quintile becomes 10.0% while the share of the top quintile falls to 36.2%. This adjustment, however, probably overstates the equalizing effect of educational expenditures since higher income families are more likely to live in school districts with greater expenditures per pupil.

CONCLUSION

Although we are acutely aware of the many sources of possible bias in constructing estimates of this sort, we believe the effort to be worthwhile. While our final estimates are subject to numerous qualifications, the official estimates of the distribution of money incomes, nevertheless, appear to be far worse, at least if they are interpreted (as they generally are) as measuring income inequality in a meaningful way.

APPENDIX

An important question in adjusting for differences in family size is whether there are economies of scale involved in larger sized households. In the polar case, with extreme economies possible, the marginal cost of supporting an additional household member would be zero. This is the case that would justify the usual treatment of comparing households regardless of household size. At the other extreme, with no economies of scale possible, a four person household would require twice as much income as a two person household to enjoy the same standard of living. In this case, a measure of household income per capita should be used.

Most people would probably agree that the "truth" lies somewhere between these two positions. Nonetheless, we use a per capita adjustment for the estimates presented in Tables 7.6–7.8. Our reasons for using this procedure are mainly computational simplicity and the absence of any acceptable measure of scale economies. In addition, any claim that there are large economies of scale in income-sharing within a household must provide some explanation of why persons do not form ever-larger households to realize these economies. In fact, in recent years, there has been a noticeable tendency toward the formation of smaller sized household units. In any event, we do not mean to suggest that there are no economies possible, but we do believe it is possible that they are small enough to neglect, at least as a first approximation.

A very different approach to this question emphasizes the welfare significance of decisions to change household size. It is sometimes pointed out that a decision to have children reduces per capita household income but increases welfare. Of course, this may be true for the parents, but it seems to neglect the welfare of the child as an independent entity within the household unit. Moreover, it is easy to construct examples which suggest a bias in the opposite direction. Divorce is also frequently voluntary. When people are divorced, the two resultant households have lower incomes than the initial household despite the presumption that they are better off. In this case, using per capita household income is clearly preferable to relying on total household income.

These examples tend to illustrate some of the murky issues involved in attempting to adjust for differences in household size. It may be best to view the per capita adjustment as identifying the easily measurable goods and services available per person in the household rather than as having any definite connection with welfare in a subjective sense.

Now let us turn to the adjustment for differences in labor supply. Following Gary Becker (1965), most analysts have chosen to use a person's wage rate to estimate the value of leisure time. For our purposes, an important issue is whether the market wage rate or net wage rate should be employed. (The net wage rate is the market wage rate times one minus the marginal tax rate.) Several economists have argued in favor of using the net wage rate, reasoning that individuals equate their marginal rate of substitution between income and leisure to the net wage rate and not the market wage rate. In spite of the plausibility of this position, we believe the market wage rate should be used to value leisure.

In Figure 7A.1, YN is the before-tax–before-transfer budget constraint. It is assumed that two individuals, A and B, both face the same market wage rate, so the constraint YN applies to both. Because of differing preferences, B chooses to work more than A, earning a money income of DL_2 compared to EL_1 for A. In the absence of any taxes or transfers, most economists would agree that the real incomes of A and B are equal. For our measures of income to reflect this, it is necessary to add to A's money income an estimate of the value of L_2L_1 hours of additional leisure enjoyed by A. Using the market wage rate to value this leisure yields CD; these are simply the additional earnings A could realize if he worked the same number of hours as B. Adding the value of leisure, CD, to A's money income, EL_1, yields DL_2 as the estimate of A's total income. By valuing leisure at the market wage rate in this case, we arrive at the correct conclusion that A and B have equal incomes of DL_2.

Now suppose that the government adopts a negative income tax which shifts

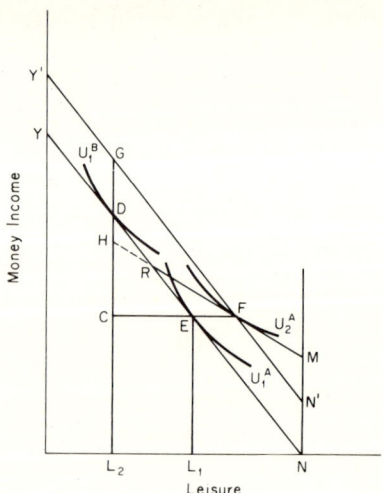

Figure 7A.1.

the constraint to *YRM*, and *A* attains a new equilibrium at point *F*. *A* now consumes *CF* more leisure than *B*, and his net wage rate is now lower because of the marginal tax rate implicit in the negative income tax. How should we value the consumption of *CF* hours of additional leisure by *A*? If we use the net wage rate as reflected in the slope of the *RM* portion of the budget constraint, this leisure would be valued at *HC*. *A*'s total income is then estimated to be HL_2, lower than *B*'s income of DL_2. However, this is clearly incorrect: If *A* and *B* initially had equal real incomes and, after the *NIT* transfer, *A* is better off than initially, he now has a higher real income than *B*.

The correct way to value *A*'s leisure time is to use his market wage, as shown by the slope of *Y'N'* which passes through point *F*. The value of *CF* in leisure is then *GC* which, when added to *A*'s money income of CL_2, measures his total real income as GL_2. Thus, *A*'s total income, GL_2, is now higher than *B*'s total income, DL_2, by the amount of the transfer received by *A*, *GD*. This makes sense. If *A* and *B* initially had identical real incomes, and *A* receives a transfer of *GD*, he then has an income of *GD* above *B*'s. Note that this procedure does not take account of the welfare cost of the transfer. *A* is not as well-off as he would be if given an unrestricted cash transfer of *GD*. Nonetheless, the welfare costs of taxes and transfers are commonly ignored in studies of income distribution and for reasonably persuasive reasons. Not only are these welfare costs small relative to the sizes of taxes and transfers, but they are virtually impossible to estimate and allocate among income classes with any accuracy. In any event, we hope this example makes it clear that it is inappropriate to use net wage rates.

The really difficult issue here is to estimate the market wage rates to use in valuing the leisure of different adults. (We apply this adjustment only for persons 18 years of age or older.) Many adults do not work at all so it is impossible to use each person's revealed market wage rate. The expedient we adopt here, although far from perfect, is as follows: Using the before-tax–before-transfer ranking, we calculate the before-tax labor income per hour of work for each quintile. The wage rate for each quintile is then assumed to apply to every adult in that quintile, with the exception of adults in the lowest quintile for whom a different procedure was employed.[5] The wage rates calculated in this way are $2.00, $4.76, $6.36, $7.49, and $10.31 for each quintile, from lowest to highest. It will be noted that the $2.00 wage rate used for the lowest quintile is below the effective minimum wage rate of $2.65 in 1976.[6]

It is easy to see that this procedure is inexact. There is no necessary reason for an adult whose total household income places him in a certain quintile to be able to work at a wage rate equal to the average of all working adults in that quintile. Yet it is far from clear in what direction this procedure biases the results. Our major concern is with the bottom quintile where relative labor supply is the lowest. In some plausible cases, $2.00 per hour greatly understates the value of leisure here: consider college students and persons retired from productive jobs. On the other hand, it is probably equally true that $2.00 overstates the value of leisure for those unable to work or involuntarily unemployed.[7] On average, we believe that using a wage rate 25% below the minimum wage for the lowest quintile is not likely to overstate the value of leisure to any significant degree.

REFERENCES

Becker, G. S. A theory of the allocation of time. *The Economic Journal*, September 1965, pp. 493-517.
Browning, E. K. The burden of taxation. *Journal of Political Economy*, August 1978, 649-671.
Business Week, Egalitarianism: Threat to a free market? December 1, 1975, p. 62.

[5] The estimated before-tax labor income per hour of work in the lowest quintile on this calculation turned out to be $0.60. This figure is implausibly low and reflects, we believe, significant underreporting of labor income in the lowest quintile. (The reported payroll taxes also turned out to be twice as large as they could possibly have been if the reported labor income were correct.) Using the before-tax–after-transfer ranking, the before-tax labor income per hour of work for the lowest quintile was estimated to be $2.50. As a somewhat arbitrary compromise, we chose a figure of $2.00 per hr.

[6] The official minimum wage was $2.35 in 1976. Workers, however, would have had to generate a before-tax labor income of about $2.65 an hr to be paid $2.35 an hr because the employer must pay payroll taxes and indirect taxes of about 12% on the before-tax labor income.

[7] Actually, even for those involuntarily unemployed, it can be argued that leisure should be valued at their potential market wage. Involuntary unemployment can be thought of as the result of a high marginal tax rate on earnings and, as argued above, it is still the before-tax wage rate that is relevant.

Business Week, Egalitarianism: Threat to a free market? December 1, 1975, p. 62.

Commager, H. S. Twelve years of Roosevelt, In E. C. Rozwenc (Ed.), *The New Deal: Revolution or evolution?* Boston: D. C. Heath, 1949, p. 27.

Economic Report of the President, 1978. Washington, D.C.: United States Government Printing Office.

Facts and Figures on Government Finance, 1977, Tax Foundation Inc., p. 218.

Hacker, L. M. "The third American revolution," In E. C. Rozwenc (Ed.), *The New Deal: Revolution or Evolution?* Boston: D. C. Heath and Company, 1949, p. 27.

Musgrave, R. A., Case, K. E. and Leonard, H. The distribution of fiscal burdens and benefits. *Public Finance Quarterly*, 1974, *2*, 259-311.

Pechman, J. A., and Okner, B. A. *Who bears the tax burden?* Washington, D.C.: Brookings Institution, 1974.

Discussion

THOMAS E. BORCHERDING

Browning and Johnson (B-J) have used sound economics and clever arithmetic to show us that income is more equally distributed than the purveyors of conventional wisdom at the Brookings Institution and the University of Wisconsin's Institute for Research on Poverty would have us believe. B-J's accomplishments, developing a theoretically consistent model of sales tax incidence and applying it to the transfer component of incomes (while adjusting for the nonmarket value of leisure), are difficult tasks. Any criticisms I offer must be weighed against the admiration I feel for their significant contribution to our understanding of how income actually is distributed in the United States.

Their results are fascinating. They remind us of what we evidently have forgotten. To wit, a general sales tax burdens not the consumer but the factor that produces the goods and services covered. This theorem, first developed in the United States by Harry Gunnison Brown and separately by Frederic Benham in Britain in the 1930s, has since been refined by Earl Rolph, Arnold Harberger, Peter Mieszkowski, Charles McClure, and by Browning (1978) himself in a recent paper in the *Journal of Political Economy* titled "The Burden of Taxation." Essentially, this literature says that the introduction of a perfectly general *ad valo-*

rem tax covering every conceivable margin of choice and yielding the same revenue as a displaced lump sum levy or poll tax will not (neglecting differential income effects) disturb final product prices. Furthermore, even if such generality is not universal and prices of commodities change, the level of prices will be unaffected except as the velocity of monetary circulation or money supply is altered. Thus, consumers whose incomes are determined in whole or part by transfers avoid all or some of a sales tax. This means that the greater the proportion of income that is determined by transfers, the less of the sales tax burden is borne.

To believe otherwise, B-J remind us, is to assert two things: (*a*) the sales tax raises *all* prices, and, (*b*) as a result, the real value of transfers is *allowed* to decline. The first condition requires that the behavior of velocity and/or the money supply be more consistent with a Post-Keynesian view of economic man than most of us here would find paradigmatically acceptable.[1] The second condition suggests that public decisions are not homogeneous of degree zero in money prices and nominal incomes, that is, they are subject to a money illusion. Both of these are inconsistent with our general view of persons taken in groups as maximizing stable objective functions. For these technical reminders alone, we should be most grateful to the authors and to Browning, in particular, as I suspect that everyone else at the Conference subscribed to the Musgrave-Pechman's (and in Canada, Gillespie's) view that the sales tax is a regressive levy heretofore.

However, the authors have done more than use the corrected general equilibrium theory of tax incidence to question the accepted fiscal wisdom. Using 1976 data based on the Census of Population Survey and Mathematica Policy Research's (CPS-MPS) analysis, they have recalculated the burden of the sales tax in a more-or-less precise fashion and have shown that it is highly progressive with respect to income. That alone is a weighty contribution.

Suppose, however, we admit the incontrovertible truth, namely, that some final goods and services are not subject to the sales tax. Love-making, prayer (as a consumer good, not as an intermediate input), the fellowship of good friends and other such leisure-time activities are exempted, as are a whole host of exempted illicit activities to be discussed below vis-à-vis the income tax. We should predict that, if they are all lumped into one category, untaxed commodities, a sales tax will cause more of them and less of the non-exempted bundle to be produced. Browning's recent article (Browning, 1978) says that as long as fac-

---

[1] To be a perfectly general tax, the services of money, M_1 through M_n, would have to be taxed too. This would speed up velocity as individuals looked for untaxed but substitutable assets to hold. Since, however, all money services *and* their substitutes would necessarily be covered by the tax, no profit could be made by such a recombination of assets. If the services of money and all their substitutes are exempted as not being final consumer goods, then, of course, there is no substitution effect and velocity is unaffected.

tor proportions in the two sectors are about the same, there will be no effect on relative factor prices as consumers and producers attempt to evade and avoid the sales tax. However, assuming, as is standard, that production in both sectors is of the linear homogeneous variety, similar factor intensities imply (as Browning explicitly recognizes) that marginal costs are unaffected with respect to changes in the composition of output. We should be skeptical about assuming constant marginal costs, even for purposes of first approximation prediction, since this strong assumption is unnecessary.

Instead, we should ask what goods and services are likely to be exempted from sales tax? The first answer is that group of commodities whose consumption or exchange the State finds difficult or impossible to monitor. With the possible exception of owner-occupied housing, these goods and services are where "firm" scale economies are decidedly minimal.[2] Most likely these goods and services are relatively labor intensive as compared to the non-exempted sector; thus the sales tax encourages the expansion of the former and contraction of the latter, raising the capital–labor ratios in both. Therefore, the net effect of exemptions is to increase the returns to labor relative to capital and, as a result, to raise the income of the bottom quintiles relative to the top one. The presence of exempted commodities probably strengthens the findings of B–J. Of course, this means that the relative prices of the two "composites" change favoring those who spend a proportionally larger share of their income on the exempted bundle of commodities. I suspect that this relative price effect is neutral at the worst and perhaps even helps the poorest vis-à-vis the wealthiest one-fifth of income receivers.

A slightly different point comes to mind regarding the income tax burden. What of the presence of that huge segment of the economy the *Wall Street Journal* calls the "subterranean economy" and which Peter Gutmann (1977) claims is at least one-tenth of the Gross National Product (GNP)? In this cash-only sector, the Internal Revenue Service (IRS) investigator finds great difficulty in assessing taxes. Again common sense suggests that these subterranean commodities are like those exempted by the sales tax in that their production is more labor intensive than those in the legitimate economy. Since the presence of income taxes causes the ratio of subterranean to legitimate activities to rise, this, too, should raise the capital–labor ratio in both sectors and, as a result, wages should increase relative to returns on capital. Again, this strengthens B–J's findings.[3]

---

[2] As many of the inputs used to produce housing are taxed, the non-exempted fraction of the total cost is perhaps only one-half the *stock* value of the house. Thus, only around one-half of the value of the final service is exempt. Other consumer durables are almost totally non-exempt at the time of their sale as assets. Thus, exempting their service flows at home is necessary to avoid double taxation of the benefits.

[3] B–J have correctly treated leisure as a valuable commodity, but they have not questioned the effects of its sales and income tax exemption on income distribution. Again, if we view

A major concern, however, is that the CPS–MPS data used by B–J do not permit more than one-half of government expenditures to be allocated among the five classes of income earners. This implicitly assumes that this non-imputed residual is distributed proportionally to tax–transfer adjusted incomes. This may be the case, but I very much doubt it. This residual—highways, parks and recreation, fire, police, public health and education, and just about everything besides the dole, social security, and hospital–health care—is in all probability, very regressively distributed. Recall, for example, the famous Hansen–Weisbrod (1969) study on the distribution of public university and college education in California that showed the chief beneficiaries of public higher education to be the children of the middle- and upper middle-classes (the top two quintiles in the B–J study). On the same topic Gordon Tullock (1971) claims that the middle and upper income groups use the expenditures side of the fiscal process to achieve what the courts would have found unconstitutionally discriminatory on the tax side.

Furthermore, the in-cash and in-kind transfers that CPS and MPR allocated to the five income classes are dramatically overstated. The "brokerage" fees levied by government bureaucrats—up to $0.90 on the dollar according to Moynihan (1973)—are very high in the case of welfare. Further, in-kind benefits measured at factor prices overstate the value received by recipients for the well-known reason that gifts-in-kind are less valuable than in-cash and, in addition, because government programs are scandalously inefficient in terms of supply cost per unit of output. When recipient "qualification" costs are also considered, it seems only prudent to reduce the value of transfers by one-third to one-half.[4] Such a reduction would decrease the degree of income equality substantially from that of B–J's findings.[5]

---

leisure as an activity using labor and capital but in labor–capital proportions greater than for non-leisure activities, it should follow that leisure's tax exemption raises wages and adds to the overall equality in income distribution.

[4] Clarkson (1975) in his study of food stamps, gives a good example of exactly what I have in mind. He found that it took roughly $1.25 of budget to distribute $1.00 of stamps to recipients. These stamps, in turn, had a value of only $0.75 to the users. Thus, for every one dollar budgeted, for this program, only $0.50 in real terms went to the putative beneficiaries. Actually, this figure is too high because the costs of qualifying for eligibility in the program, to say nothing of the efforts in queuing up, are not included. Tullock has facetiously referred to this phenomenon as Friedman II's law. Friedman II refers to David, son of Milton, who proclaims not only that the government cannot produce goods and services efficiently because of well-known institutional impedimentia, but that it cannot even give these goods and services (or straight income) away without significant losses in the procedure. Almost all objective students of the War on Poverty agree with this observation. Moynihan (1973), even more cynically but no less perspicaciously, notes that the chief beneficiaries of the poverty battle have been social workers whose incomes have risen more than twice as fast (in real terms) as those of all workers over the last 15 years.

[5] There is a nice Lancaster–Lipsey logic to arguing that, since welfare losses due to "market failures" are not subtracted from factor incomes, we ought not delete governmental

On another issue, their calculation of an individual's income as a member of a household, I must also demur. In the Appendix, B-J point out that income might involve economies of scale in household consumption, but they dismiss this on the grounds that, if this were so, nothing would limit the household's size. Given this reasoning, they assume that the goods and services consumed by the household unit are purely divisible among its members in consumption. Their calculation of individual income from that of the household considerably equalizes the distribution of income since there are twice as many individuals in the top fifth average household (3.3 people) as there are in those of the poorest quintile (1.6 persons). The presence of consumption economies would moderate this finding.

Yet consumption economies exist. Food, liquor, paper goods and possibly towels (but not necessarily sheets) are easily divisible in consumption, but one does not normally put another bathroom, refrigerator, or television into the home after an additional person joins the household. In fact, one wonders why, if joint economies of some sort do not exist, households are so anthropologically pervasive? It cannot be merely for economics of team production because households exist even when members do not specialize in various aspects of household production.

Futhermore, the existence of such economies does not imply that the household enlarges to include the Family of Man in one glorious, Maoist commune. This is shown by the assumption of diminishing returns, with respect to household size, (*a*) of measured household income and (*b*) of jointness in consumption.

Let me offer a model that demonstrates the existence of a determinant sized household, but which also permits a first approximation estimation of the economies of joint consumption. Let y be the real income captured from the household's measured income, I, and let N be the size of the household in numbers of person. Thus, if one assumes

$$y = I/N^\alpha \qquad (1)$$
$$(1 > \alpha > 0)$$

where α is the coefficient of publicness, an individual's share of household in-

---

waste either. This has no great appeal to me, however. The losses to the "market failures" are probably proportional to private spending so this would not change distribution markedly from what is observed except to favor the very poor ever so slightly since so much of their "spending" is on government in-kind transfers. The costs of the governmental waste, however, are of a wholly greater order of magnitude (rectangles *plus* triangles) than the former (largely triangles) and, disproportionately, burden the poorer groups. Putting it quite directly, if all the transfer programs are counted as income, the poor would be almost as wealthy as the average person; casual observation tells us this is patent nonsense.

come is found simply by multiplying I by the reciprocal of N^α. (α cannot exceed 1 or the household would break up into a more efficient, smaller size.)

Further, assume that the relationship of I to N is positive and increasing, but that diminishing returns exist so that

$$I = F(N) \qquad (2)$$
$$(F_N > 0 \text{ and } F_{NN} < 0)$$

In addition, assume that jointness in consumption also diminishes with the size of the unit. At $N = 1$, α is 0, but α rises thereafter so that

$$\alpha = a + bN \qquad (3)$$

Now α obviously is 0 when N is 1, so it follows that a equals $-b$ and Eq. (3) can be rewritten

$$\alpha = b(N - 1) \qquad (4)$$

If households attempt to "find" their optimal size, N^*, real income is maximized when

$$\frac{dy}{dN} = \frac{\frac{dI}{dN}N^\alpha - \frac{dN^\alpha}{dN}I}{(N^\alpha)^2} = 0$$

or

$$\alpha^* = \epsilon/(1 + \delta^* \ln N^*)$$

(ϵ is the elasticity of I and δ^* is the elasticity of α both with respect to N. Note by Eq. (2) it is obvious that $\delta^* = N^*/N^* - 1$).

Given that $N^* = 3$ by casual observation of the average household's "revealed preference" in the United States in recent years,[6] δ^* is 1.5. Assuming $\epsilon = 0.5$ (purely by guess) it follows that $\alpha^* = 0.19$. α's for N's other than N^* can then be calculated[7] as $\alpha = (\alpha^*/N^* - 1)(N - 1)$. (Recall $a = -b$ so when $\alpha = 0.19$ and $N = 3$ it follows that $b = a^*/N^* - 1 = .095$.)

---

[6] It is clear that there are extreme costs to achieving $N^* = 3$, or the observed dispersion of N around N^* would not exist. I am assuming, however, that the average household's size, $N = 3$, approximates this desideratum.

[7] It is interesting to note that α does not become one until the household becomes 11.5 persons! Of course, if ϵ rises, say to 0.75, α^* rises to 0.28 and $\alpha = 1$ is associated with a much smaller household of 8.1 persons. Thus, both α^* and N ($\alpha = 1$) are very sensitive to

For the poorest fifth with an average household size of 1.6 persons, the reciprocal of N^α is 0.97, that is, individual income is only 3% less than household income. For the richest quintile with 3.3 persons per household $1/N^\alpha$ is 0.77, that is, the individual's income is 23% less than the household income.

It is interesting to note how this changes the distribution of *individual* income from B-J's estimate. The authors claim that, using unadjusted household income, the ratio of the highest to lowest quintile is around eight. Using their assumption that $\alpha = 1$ for both groups it follows then that the ratio of highest to lowest income per person falls to below 4-to-1. However, if my "guestimated" N^α's are employed, the ratio of real incomes would be of little over 6-to-1. This is 50% less equality than B-J found. Of course, more precise measures of α will give better estimates, but clearly α ought to lie somehwere between 0 and 1. It must follow then that the ratio of real income per person must lie somewhere between those found on a pure household basis ($\alpha = 0$) and B-J's version ($\alpha = 1$). My intermediate ratio is probably not too far from the truth.

Unfortunately, even if the authors could adjust their numbers perfectly, they still could not answer two important questions. First how would the distribution appear with very different sets of taxes and transfers, and, second, is the distribution of income really an interesting question? However, for the more limited purpose of their study in scrutinizing the actual distribution of income given the existing set of fiscal conditions, B-J have succeeded admirably. Their research destroys another myth, and, for this, we are in their debt.

REFERENCES

Browning, E. K. The burden of taxation. *Journal Political Economy*, Aug. 1978, *86*, 649-72.

Clarkson, K. W. *Food stamps and nutrition*. Washington, D.C.: American Enterprise Institute, 1975.

Gutmann, P. The subterranean economy. *Financial Analysts Journal*, Nov. 1977, *33*, 26-27.

Hansen, W. Lee, & Weisbrod, B. A. *Benefits, costs and finance of public higher education.* Chicago: Markham Publishing, 1969.

Moynihan, D. P. *The politics of a guaranteed income: The Nixon administration and the Family Assistance Plan.* New York: Random House, 1973.

Tullock, G. The charity of the uncharitable. Dec. 1971, *9*, 379-392.

---

the size of ϵ. If ϵ is 0.75, that is, a doubling of the household's size raises its claims on measurable real income by 75%, α^* rises to 0.28. α for $N = 1.6$ persons then becomes 0.08, and α is 0.32 when $N = 3.3$ people. Therefore, the ratio of per person income between the uppermost and lowest fifths is 5.7. With an ϵ of 0.50, my original assumption, this ratio was 6.3. Thus, a 40% change in the estimate for ϵ yields only a 10% change in the ratio of "true" per capita incomes. This suggests that the procedure I have employed is rather robust and ought to be pursued somewhat further on both theoretical and empirical grounds.

Subject Index

A

Act for Punishment of Rogues, Vagabonds, and Sturdy Beggars, 49
Adamnson Act, 43
AFDC, 49-50
Agricultural
 cooperatives, 38-39
 Market Act, 38
Agriculture, 3, 4, 9, 38-39
American Association of Public Accountants, 114-115
American Institute of Public Accountants, 115
Antitrust Division of the Justice Department, 48, 68
Antitrust laws and policies, 39, 41-42, 48, 52, 67-71, 77

B

Bank(s)
 acts of 1933 and 1935, 47, 93, 98
 deposits in, federal insurance of, 18, 80, 82-83, 88-89, 93-95, 98
 failures of, 79, 81-82, 88, 94, 97
 panics, 3, 5, 88, 94
 reserves of, 85
Banking
 reform of, 77-99
 regulation of, 17, 80-82, 87-89, 93-97
 system, 16, 83, 89
Bureau of the Budget, 45

C

Child Labor Act, 43
Civil Aeronautics Board, 47, 49, 69
Clayton Act, 42
Collective bargaining, 41-44, 77
Commodity Credit Corporation, 38
Competition, 10, 48, 59, 76, 102-103, 116-117
Corporate Excise Tax Law, 114
Credit, 83, 85, 87, 98-99, 108

161

D

Depression, Great, 4, 14, 18, 22, 28, 32, 44, 52, 58–60, 65, 75, 79, 85, 130
Deregulation, 22, 118, 124
Discretionary power, 102, 106–107, 109, regulation and, 118
Dollar, the, 8, 24, 79

E

Economic constitution, 13–29
Economics, 24–25, 28–29
  free-market, 32, 87
  Keynesian, 18–19, 23–24, 28, 154
Economy, American, 1, 3, 10, 16, 83–84
Employment, 3, 6, 15, 17, 19, 23–24, 33, 38, 44, 59
  Act of 1946, 49, 52
Erdman Act, 43
Export–Import Bank, 38

F

Farm Security Administration, 47
Federal
  assistance programs, 3
  budget, 7
    balanced, 18, 23–24
    deficits of, 7–9, 24, 33
  Communications Commission, 47
  Deposit Insurance Corporation, 82, 88, 94
  expenditures, 7, 34–41, 57, 60, 129–130
  Farm
    Board, 38
    Loan Act, 39
  fiscal policy, 6, 18, 24, 33
  Housing Administration, 39
  National Mortgage Association, 39
  Reserve
    Board, 17, 47, 80–82, 85, 89, 95–96
    system, 3–6, 8, 10, 14, 16, 28, 33, 79–81, 86, 89, 93–94, 97–99
  Shipping Board, 40
  Trade Commission, 68–69, 71, 111
Food and Drug Administration, 60
Fraud, securities, 108–109
Free-enterprise system, 3–4, 52, 64
Full Employment Act of 1946, 19

G

Gallatin Plan, 39
Gold
  reserves, 6, 16, 79, 85
  standard, 4, 15–16, 28, 112
Goldsborough bill, 16–17
Governments, state and local, 3, 32, 38–39, 58, *see also* Federal
Great Society, 7, 19, 22
Gross National Product, 1–2, 6, 76, 84, 155

H

Home Owners Loan Corporation, 6
Household composition and income distribution, 142–151, 157–159

I

Income
  distribution of, 34, 130, 136–137, 141, 153–159
  inequality, 130, 142–148
    evaluation of, 142–148
  taxes and transfers and, 129–159
Inflation, 7–10, 19, 23, 33, 59, 89–90
Inland Waterways Corporation, 40
Insurance
  government, bank deposits and, 18, 80, 82–83, 88–89, 93–95, 98
  social, 49–52, 57
  unemployment, 129–132
Intercoastal Shipping Act of 1938, 40
Interest rates, regulation of, 24, 79, 81, 85–87, 89–90, 93, 95–96, 98
Interstate Commerce Act, 40

K

Keynes, Lord, 1, 29
Keynesian economics, 18–19, 23–24, 28, 154

L

Labor unions, 8, 15, 41–44, 57
Laissez-faire, 13–14, 52
Law, common, 41–42, 44–46

Subject Index

Leisure, value of, 149-151
Lever Food Control Act, 39

M

Market, the, 9, 14-16, 19, 22-25, 28-29
    31, 48, 60-61, 98
  crises and regulation of, 102, 104, 107,
    114
  failures and regulation of, 102-107,
    109-110, 114, 123-125
McNary-Haugen bills, 38
Medicare, 50
Merchant Marine Acts, 40
Miller-Tydings Act, 48, 65
Monetary
  crises, 1-11
  policy, 4, 6, 9, 14-18, 28, 33, 81-82,
    84-87, 89
Money supply, 4-5, 8-9, 17, 83-86, 89, 94,
    97-99, 154

N

National Banking System, 39
National Industrial Recovery Act, 58-59
National Labor Relations Board, 41, 43, 58
National Maritime Commission, 40
National Recovery Administration, 81
National Waterways Commission, 40
New Deal, 3, 6-7, 13-29, 31-62, 64-67, 73,
    88, 93, 96-97, 101, 108-109,
    129-130
New York Stock Exchange, 102, 111-113,
    115-118

O

Office of Economic Opportunity, 45, 47
Office of Management and Budget, 68

P

Panama Canal Act, 40
Patman Bonus bill, 17
Price
  discrimination and, 64, 67-68, 70-71,
    75-76
  index and, consumer, 1, 16-17, 133

  levels of, 1, 9, 18-19, 24, 29, 64
  stability of, 33
Proposition 13, 10
Public works, 36, 47, 129
Pure Food and Drug Act, 60

R

Railway Labor Act, 43
Reconstruction Finance Corporation, 6, 39
  Mortgage Company, 39
Regulation, 4-7, 9, 13, 21, 31-62
  theories of, 101-127
Regulatory
  agencies, federal, 44-49, 52, 57, 101,
    107-108, 115-117, 125
  reform, 64, 67-71, 102
    Securities and Exchange Commission
      and, 115-119
Rivers and Harbors Act, 40
Robinson-Patman Act, 48, 63-67
Rural Electrification Act, 49

S

Securities and Exchange Act, 93, 98, 108,
    111, 124, 127
Securities and Exchange Commission,
    47-49, 101-127
  regulatory reform by, 115-119
Sherman Act, 42, 44, 71
Shipping Act of 1916, 40
Silver, 35, 79
  Purchase Act of 1934, 35
Small business, 63-73, 75
  Administration, 47
Socialism, 4, 15, 22, 41
Social Security, 22-23, 50-51, 53, 129,
    133, 135, 141, 156
Statute of Artificers and Apprentices, 44,
    49
Stock market, 98, 108, 114
  prices, 4, 108, 112
Subsidies
  federal, 31, 34-41, 47, 57-58, 60
  food, 129, 156
Supreme Court, 22, 28

T

Tax

Tax (cont.)
  burdens of, distribution of, 132–137
  income, 49, 51–52
    negative, 141, 149–150
    progressive, 134–137
  property, 10, 35
  revolt, 9–10
  sales, 132–134, 136, 153–155
  system, the, 132–137
Taxes, 22, 33, 130
  transfers and, 130, 137–142
    income inequality and, 129–159
Transfers, and income redistribution, 134, 137–141

U

Unemployment, 3, 5–6, 15, 24, 38, 49–52, 59, 75, 151
  insurance, 129, 132
Unions, see Labor unions
United States Housing Corporation, 39

W

Wage
  minimum, 25
  price controls and, 8–10, 15, 17, 25, 89
Wagner Act, 41, 59
War
  Finance Corporation, 39
  Labor Board, 43
Welfare, 7, 49, 76, 129, 156
  expenditures, 129–130, 150
  family size and, 149
  programs, 129–130

Soc
HC
106.3
R464

DATE DUE

~~T.R. APR 8 1983~~	~~NOV 21 1994~~
~~LR DEC 12 1984~~	JUL 1 8 2009
~~CT JUN 17 1986~~	
~~CV DEC 07 1986~~	
~~CT DEC 30 1986~~	
~~CT MAR 31 1987~~	
~~DEC 9 1988~~	
~~OCT 31 1994~~	
~~DEC 12 1994~~	

MP 728